The Story of
Annie Armstrong

Cathy Butler

Woman's Missionary Union®
Birmingham, Alabama

Woman's Missionary Union, SBC
P. O. Box 830010
Birmingham, AL 35283-0010

For more information, visit our Web site at www.wmu.com or call
1-800-968-7301.

Dewey Decimal Classification: 922.6
Subject Headings: ARMSTRONG, ANNIE WALKER
                  WOMAN'S MISSIONARY UNION—HISTORY

Design by Janell E. Young
Cover design by Cheryl Totty

ISBN: 1-56309-861-X
W043106•0704•2.5M1

Contents

Introduction

Everybody loves a hero. From Deborah the prophetess of Israel to modern-day shuttle astronauts, soldiers, and firefighters, women have shown they can be heroes. They have proven they have the courage, strength, boldness, and intellect to lead in tough situations. There are plenty of other people in today's sound-bite world that also try to prove how fearless, cunning, or adventurous they are, hoping for a moment's glory. That, perhaps, is the main difference between the fame seekers and the true heroes. The women we think of as heroes engage in great acts in order to fulfill a great duty, whether it is furthering humanity's knowledge of outer space or pulling someone from a burning car.

If, then, achieving great things out of a clear sense of duty is one mark of a hero, Annie Armstrong belongs in any list of women heroes. She didn't have superpowers, but she worked at almost a superhuman pace. She didn't know martial arts, but she knew how to fight for the cause of missions. She didn't wear a space suit or armor; she did her heroic work in long dresses and a bonnet. She didn't carry a gun; she could defend herself with her pen and writing stationery. She didn't conquer cities; she conquered a spirit of apathy and confusion by shaping—with the help of her co-workers—a confederation of women's mission societies into Woman's Missionary Union® (WMU®).

Knowledge of this great woman's life has fallen away through the years. Many people think she was a home missionary because the Annie Armstrong Easter Offering® for Home (now North American) Missions was named for her. She was not a missionary. Nor was she Lottie Moon's mother! In order to help renew knowledge and interest in Annie, WMU has brought out this new biography of her life. It is based upon the incomparable work *Annie Armstrong: Dreamer in Action* by Bobbie Sorrill (Patterson).

Since this book reads more like someone telling a story than a scholarly text, you as the reader might wonder, "How do I know what part is true?" The answer is that the story of Annie's life is told as accurately as possible. Any words attributed to her, either spoken or written, are her actual words. No fictional dialogue was written for her. But, since we can hardly hope to find complete records of everything said by every family member, servant, or church member, how could the book be interesting without allowing the characters to speak outside of what is recorded in WMU meetings? To solve this dilemma, dialogue was created for anonymous servants and church members who voice opinions and questions that would have naturally been voiced in Annie's day.

Likewise, anything quoted in a letter to or from Annie comes from a documented historical source. And, since this is a historical work, readers should take into account that certain terms were in use in the 1890s that are not considered correct today; for example, *American Indian*. Annie Armstrong had a tremendous love and concern for Native American tribes. Hearing of their needs and mistreatment was one of the things that spurred her interest in home missions. When she spoke and wrote of them, she called them *Indians*. The use of the term *Native American* had simply not come into broad use when Annie was living. For the sake of historical accuracy, *Indian* is used in telling her story, although WMU and the writer realize that use of this term is outmoded in the twenty-first century.

The same argument can be made for certain attitudes Annie had concerning the role of women. Some may find her viewpoints about women speaking in mixed groups (or not having her picture made for fear some man would carry it into a saloon) to be out of sync with modern life. Again, to be historically accurate, Annie's attitudes must be presented honestly. She should not be judged by twenty-first-century manners. And, she was such a progressive, forward-thinking person, creating places of leadership for women who came after her, that it is to be hoped people would see the entire picture of what this remarkable woman did, rather than the few things she refused to do.

Finally, it should be pointed out that Annie Armstrong, while an amazing woman, was not perfect. She was thin-skinned and demanding, among other things. She was an imperfect person, and she showed through her life what an imperfect person who has dedicated herself heart and soul to serving God can accomplish. If she had been obsessed with making money for herself, she could probably have become a millionaire. If she had craved praise and attention, she could have probably conquered Baltimore society. But, like a hero, she wanted to give all her gifts and abilities to fulfilling her duty. And generations of missionaries, churches, and Southern Baptist women have been blessed by it.

1
The Early Years

1850

On a hot summer day in suburban Baltimore, a tired young woman and her new baby lay resting in a comfortable bedroom. The mother's straight dark hair was wet with sweat, her gentle face still lined with the pain of childbirth. But she was happy. The Lord had delivered her of a healthy daughter, her third in 5 years.

Mary Armstrong smiled as she thought of little James, just born in April of the previous year. His reign as the baby of the family was over, but his place as only son was still unchallenged, for now.

She cradled her new daughter, and noted with some pleasure—which she hoped was not prideful—that the baby looked like her, with round dark eyes and full lips. Three-year-old Alice looked more like her father. She had the same long face, wide mouth, and deep-set eyes.

"Will you be tall like your father, or small like your mother, little Annie?" she whispered to her newborn.

The baby yawned in answer and fell asleep. Her mother, still exhausted from her labor, rested too.

News spread quickly through both the Armstrong and the Walker families that Mary and James had another daughter. Since their marriage in 1844, the couple had been busy growing their family. Mary Elizabeth, nicknamed Mamie, was born in 1845; followed by Alice in 1846; then James John in 1849; and now this child, who made her appearance today, July 11, 1850.

What will you name the baby? was the question of the day.

"Her name is Annie, after my sister," Mary replied. "And her middle name is Walker, after my family."

It was no surprise that Mary named the baby after her sister Ann, who was only 1 year older than Mary in the Walker brood of nine girls and eight boys. But what a shame Annie's Grandmother Walker had not lived to see her. Mary had buried her mother only 1 short year after her marriage to James Dunn Armstrong.

"Your husband has taken out an extra-large advertisement in the *Baltimore Sun* for the tobacco shop today," someone mentioned.

"It's an important day," Mary said smiling.

1852

Mary Armstrong moved through the house with quiet, sad steps. Her body swayed with the weight of yet another pregnancy. She was expecting her baby in three months. But this Armstrong baby would never know its father. Tall, steady, serious-faced James Armstrong was dead at age 48.

Mary had known that with a husband 18 years older than herself, she was likely to outlive him, but his illness had been so brief. . . . It was all so sudden. Now she was a 30-year-old widow with four little children and another on the way. Before James's death there had been the recent fire in Baltimore's warehouse district. Their tobacco warehouse on Cheapside Street was in the middle of the district. And there was her father's death. And the financial losses in the family business. What would she do? Where could she turn for help?

She turned to the source of all her strength in life, to God. Through the funeral and burial, through the long days and nights that followed, she prayed. Mary had been taught by her Baptist family to believe in a God Who heard and answered prayer. Since her Great-Grandfather Sater came to Maryland, her ancestors had been dedicated Christians. She would not falter from their teachings or example. While James had been a Presbyterian and she a Baptist, he had given generously to Seventh Baptist Church and to charitable causes. Now he was not beside her to help bring up their children in the Lord; it was up to her.

After William was born, there were decisions to be made. The family moved from the home at 41 North Calvert Street to a row house at 53 McCulloh Street. The front of the house boasted neither porch nor yard, just steps leading to the sidewalk and the street. But it was an upstanding neighborhood.

Life went on. Mary faithfully took her children to Seventh Baptist Church. She started them in school when the time came. People commented on what tall girls Alice and Annie were getting to be.

1858

"William's dead!" The disbelieving cry rang out through the Armstrong and Levering households. How, the grown-ups asked, how could it have happened? The children were all playing, rough and tumble yes, but that's how children play. It was just a hard push from an older playmate—but it had killed 6-year-old William.

Those who loved Mary Armstrong watched, fearful that this would be the blow from which she would not recover. Their fears were unfounded. Mary called all the children around her. She looked into their grief-stricken faces and spoke calmly, quietly through her own tears.

"Children, I do not want you to discuss the accident. I do not want you telling others which child pushed William. We will not speak of this to other people. It was an accident."

Mary buried William next to his father in Westminster Burial Grounds, and never spoke of his death again. Some hurts were too deep for words.

1861

The days slipped past and Mary bent all her considerable energy into raising her children and preparing them for what was to come. A terrible war was brewing between North and South, and Baltimore was caught in the middle, geographically and politically.

One day in April a crowd of Southern sympathizers set upon Union soldiers traveling between train stations in the city. The attack started with shouts and insults. It turned into a riot with 12 people dead and many more hurt. It was bad enough that the city was under military rule, with newspapers suppressed and an assassination threat against Mr. Lincoln. Her pastor, Dr. Fuller, and the other pastors had to be careful of what they said from the pulpit. One thoughtless word in a sermon or prayer could bring a charge of treason.

Mary found that while she could protect her children from carnage such as the riot, she could not shield them from the war completely.

"Mother, have you noticed the Cary girls' hair ribbons?" Mamie asked her mother one day.

"Why, no, I have not," Mary answered, preoccupied with the household account books. Annie watched in fascination as her mother balanced the ledgers. Numbers were so interesting. Perhaps, she thought, when she was a grown lady like her mother she could have an account book of her very own!

"They are white and red," Mamie announced in a dramatic tone. Mary looked up from her work.

"White and red?" she repeated.

Alice chimed in. "And their aprons are trimmed in red, too!"

"Are you going to let us have red and white rosettes for our hair, Mother?" asked Mamie.

"No, I think not," her mother replied, and went back to work. Mary did not like to speak against anyone and Mr. and Mrs. Cary, the parents of the ribbon-wearing girls, were also the owners of the Southern Home School, which Mamie and Alice attended. Besides being good schoolteachers, however, the Carys were Virginians with a great loyalty to the Confederate cause, a loyalty they had apparently transmitted to their daughters. Red and white were the Rebel colors, and a federal order forbade them being displayed.

"But what can the soldiers do?" Mary wondered. They couldn't very well stop a young girl and say, "You are under arrest for wearing hair ribbons and an apron!" Mary, however, could keep her daughters from engaging in such behavior, and she could teach them to treat everyone with Christian courtesy and fairness. This treatment extended to their servants, some of whom were black. Mary tried to show her girls that servants deserved the same kindness and mannerly treatment as anyone else. Some people were amused by her approach to human relations.

"My mama would never stand for me saying please and thank you to the maid like those Armstrong girls do," sneered a young Baltimore miss.

"Yes," sighed a friend. "But I've visited in their home and I can tell you, their mother doesn't stand for you *not* being kind, even to the maid."

1863

The family was moving again, to a row house at 1423 McCulloh Street.

"Oh look, Annie, there are three stories. What a lot of room we shall have!" cried Mamie. The girls stepped through the narrow front of their new home and investigated the inside. The hall had a long, winding staircase to the upper floors. Behind the staircase the house opened into a big parlor. The formal dining room was on the front of the house.

"Oh, Annie, look at the nice big kitchen!" Alice squealed. Their mother had already told them the basement, which they would reach using the outside stairs, could be the summertime kitchen. "Won't this be nice?" Alice asked.

"Uh-huh," Annie mumbled. Kitchens and cooking did not appeal to her at all.

"What's upstairs, Mother?" James asked, trying to look grown up, not childishly excited like his sisters, who were embarrassing him with their enthusiasm.

"A nice big sitting room for us, and bedrooms. And more bedrooms on the third floor," Mary answered.

"There's a dumb waiter!" Alice pulled at the contraption in the wall. "We can have our food brought up to the upper floors." Annie came alive.

"Let me see," she said. After manipulating the dumb waiter a few moments, she gave her approval. "Think how much fun this will be, Alice. I hope we live here a long time."

Mary was pleased with the new home, which brought her closer to her sister Ann Levering and her family. Mary needed her sister as never before. Ann's husband, Eugene Levering Sr., had an excellent mind for business and finance, and Mary needed to make the most out of what was left of the family fortune.

So much had happened since the sultry summer day Mary gave birth to Annie. Mary believed in counting her blessings, and they were still many. She had her extended family, especially the Leverings and their growing brood of children. She had enough money to send the girls to private school and to live quietly but comfortably, without having to leave her children and find a job.

She had her church. And she had her children: sweet Mamie, adventure-loving James, friendly Alice, . . . and Annie! Her child with clever mind, strong will, and tender heart. She didn't know what the future held for them all, but surely the Lord had work for them.

2

Dawning Interest in Missions

1868

"Well, now that Miss Mamie is married off to Mr. Levering, it's just the two younger girls with their mother," observed one woman house servant to another as they prepared the Armstrongs' breakfast a few days after the oldest Armstrong sister's wedding.

"Yes," mused the other. "Such a shame Mr. James ran away like that, him being the only living son and all. But in a city like Baltimore, around the harbor and the ships all the time, I guess adventuring at sea gets in a young man's blood."

Life had changed drastically for Mary Armstrong and her girls. The Civil War had ended, though its effects would last for years. Mamie had married her cousin, Eugene Levering Jr. James had run off to sea, leaving just Mary, Alice, and Annie in the house at 1423 McCulloh Street.

Ever the watchful and caring mother, Mary realized that average ladies were expected to live in dainty solitude until marriage or death. But who, Mary thought ruefully, would ever call Alice and Annie average ladies?

Mary straightened the lace at her collar as she dressed for Sunday morning services at Seventh Baptist Church.

There would be other times to contemplate her daughters' futures. Right now they had to get from McCulloh Street to the church, which was at Paca and Saratoga. She did not want to miss a minute of the service. Dr. Fuller was such a riveting preacher. Though he had sometimes expressed sympathy for the Confederacy, he had done all he could to keep Baltimore calm and Maryland in the Union. Above all, he had wanted peace.

And what would Southern Baptist missionaries have done without him? When the sea blockade had stopped missionaries from getting their salaries, Richard Fuller used his persuasive powers and his position as president of the Southern Baptist Convention to convince the secretary of state to allow the funds to come under a flag of truce from the Foreign Mission Board (now International Mission Board) in Richmond to him in Baltimore. A provisional Foreign Mission Board was set up in Baltimore, and it made sure the missionaries received their funds.

Mary's heart had been touched by the pastor's sermon on the day of fasting and prayer after poor President Lincoln's murder. His sermon was credited with bringing together the Baltimoreans who were divided over the war. Dr. Fuller had ended the remarkable sermon with the great Scripture passage of Ephesians 4:31–32. "Let all bitterness and wrath and anger and clamor and slander be put away from you, with all malice, and be kind to one another, tenderhearted, forgiving one another, as God in Christ forgave you." It was a masterful closing.

Yes, she thought, as she left home. There was something commanding about Dr. Fuller. Even restless Annie stayed still long enough to pay attention to his sermons!

At the beginning of services the worshippers saw the usual sight of petite Mary Armstrong walking to her pew, accompanied by her two tall, ramrod-straight daughters. It was known their mother had taught the girls grace and good posture by making them practice with broomsticks to help keep their backs straight. As respected as the Armstrongs were, it was also rumored that Mrs. Armstrong insisted that the girls learn to think, love ideas, study hard, and devote themselves to a life of service above and beyond social events. Was she not fearful, some wondered, that her daughters would end up insane or sterile from such mental exercise? At least Alice enjoyed the womanly pursuits of meal planning and housekeeping. Annie, with her unfeminine interest in business, seemed especially likely to contract brain fever.

But, Annie and Alice had flourished under their mother's encouragement and guidance. One thing that did send Mary to the Lord in prayer many times, however, was Annie's salvation. Alice had made her profession of faith and been baptized in 1864, as had Mamie. Annie went to church, memorized Scripture, and adored music, but she had not made that great step of claiming Christ as her Savior. And there was a denomination issue with her. Mary looked over at her daughter and recalled her saying firmly, and more than once, "Mother, I could be a Presbyterian or even an Episcopalian, but never a Baptist." Mary kept praying.

1870

"The religion of Jesus Christ gives peace in the midst of trouble." Dr. Fuller's deep voice with its polished Harvard inflections rolled across the congregation at Seventh Baptist Church. The truth of his words rolled into the restless heart of a 20-year-old woman sitting with her mother and sister.

Peace! Peace in the midst of trouble. Annie thought of her mother, who had endured so much and yet was not destroyed or beaten down by anything. How she had longed to be like her mother, to have what Mary Armstrong had. People did not know how Annie chafed under the limitations of her life. She feared the energy and ambition inside her might cause her to explode one day if she could find no outlet. Peace—this was what she had been searching for, and it was here all along. Annie felt the Holy Spirit open her spiritual eyes and ears. She claimed the peace of Jesus Christ.

"You shall be baptized in December, Annie," Mary said. She felt as if her heart would burst, she was so full of gratitude to God for Annie's conversion. "But . . . can you be a Baptist?"

"Oh, Mother," Annie said stoutly. "I could never be anything *but* a Baptist!"

<u>1871</u>

"The church is finished!" the Armstrongs and the Leverings rejoiced that Eutaw Place Baptist Church was ready to open for services. The church, with its steeple reaching into the sky and its lovely old-world architecture, was built not far from where the Armstrong women lived. They were prepared to become charter members, along with nearly 130 other believers.

"Who will be the pastor?" friends and neighbors asked.

"Dr. Fuller, of course," Mary answered.

While the Armstrongs loved Seventh Baptist Church, they were ready to begin services at Eutaw Place. The church offered several attractions: the opportunity to help with a new work, the nearness to home, and the presence of Dr. Fuller. And, to be honest, they agreed, it was good to be in a church where women could contribute. Their former church had allowed the female members a rigid and limited area of influence. This would not be so at Eutaw Place.

Mary, Alice, and Annie spent time considering the purchases they should make for the building. Even before services started, the women of the church had been asked to put the finishing touches on the building. They had already contributed money to pay for the building, and they gave again to furnish it. The church was as beautiful and elegant on the inside as it was on the outside. To help pay expenses, the church had agreed to adopt the rent-a-pew method. Mary rented the fifth pew from the front for her and her girls.

One morning the 35 women who had agreed to help with the furnishings met to go over their expenses. "Let's see," said one woman. "Our records show we have bought everything from carpets and furniture to tack hammers and glue."

"And we've put the hammers and glue to good use!" another joked.

"The work will be finished soon," another group member suggested.

Mary Armstrong smiled at Alice and Annie at this comment, but her good manners would not allow her to contradict the speaker. She believed, as she taught her children, that there would always be work to do for the Lord, as long as one was living. To be useful for the kingdom, with no expectation of ease or reward, was the secret to a well-lived life.

The weeks sped past. Spring came to Baltimore, making the city more beautiful than ever. Tired of being cooped up all winter, families poured into Druid Hill Park near McCulloh Street to walk the paths or watch the swans in the lake. In the pleasant twilight women again brought out straw mats to the stoops of their brick row houses. They sat on the mats in the warm evening air and visited while their children played safely in the streets.

Now that Eutaw Place was functioning, the church needed a Working Society to care for its female members and oversee the duties of the ladies' societies: the Dorcas Society, a mothers' meeting, and a sewing school. The role of president in the Working Society would be an important one. The president must be a hard worker, able to lead and coordinate, and she must have spiritual depth.

"Mary," the question soon came, "would you be willing to be the Working Society president?" To no one's great surprise, Mary said yes.

Alice and Annie watched their mother conduct quarterly meetings that reviewed and discussed the society work. Then there was the women's prayer meeting, led by Annie's friend, Jane Norris, and six committees who did everything from preparing candidates for baptism to visiting the poor. The only drawback to the work was lack of interest in missions, a subject dear to Mary's heart.

Long before becoming a charter member of Eutaw Place, Mary became involved with a woman's mission society led by the outstanding Mrs. Ann Jane Graves. Like other Baltimore Baptists, the Armstrongs knew Mrs. Graves's reputation, although she was not a member of Eutaw Place. She had been baptized in 1868 into First Baptist Church, which some people called First Female Baptist Church because at one time all the active members were women. Not only that, but women could vote and serve on committees.

Ann Jane Graves, however, was just the kind of member such a church needed. She was a brilliant woman, well-read, an author, and a strong advocate of education for women. It was not that she wanted women to be men, her admirers explained. Mrs. Graves felt that an educated woman could do a better job as a wife and mother. Mrs. Graves was herself a mother. Had not one of her children, Rosewell, gone to China as a missionary doctor when he was only 22 years old?

Indeed, Rosewell spurred his mother to organize for missions. He wrote to her of the need for a Bible woman, a Chinese woman who would take Bibles into Chinese homes and read Scripture to the women. In 1864 the women of his family began sending money to pay the salary of a Bible woman.

While he appreciated this effort, Rosewell did not let up in his efforts to remind his mother how much the China missionaries needed the support of Christian women at home. So in 1867 Mrs. Graves organized the

Female Missionary Prayer Meeting. In 1868, when the Southern Baptist Convention met in Baltimore, she was bold enough to go into the gallery as a visitor and invite the other women visitors to gather around her and read letters from missionaries and to pray for them. She then urged the women to go home and organize for missions.

Interest in missions work was gathering, and Mrs. Graves was not going to let the opportunity pass. In 1869 a Woman's Union Missionary Society missionary, Harriet Brittan, was on furlough (now stateside assignment). Mrs. Graves invited her to Baltimore. The missionary accepted the invitation, and the large audience who attended her talk was thrilled with what she said. So thrilled that in February of the next year, Baltimore had its own branch of the society, with Mrs. Graves as corresponding secretary and Corinthia Williams, the wife of First Baptist Church pastor J. W. M. Williams, as president.

"With Mother and Jane Norris both officers in Woman's Mission to Woman, the church will certainly receive missions information," the Armstrong sisters assured each other. Annie didn't realize how much Jane was going to influence both Eutaw Place and herself in the cause of missions.

1872

"Annie, Dr. Graves has asked me to be his wife." Jane Norris's announcement to her friend meant more than just happy news of a young woman's engagement. It meant, Annie knew, that she might never see Jane again. Mrs. Graves's son had returned from the missions field of China, a widower looking for a wife. Dr. Graves intended to return to China . . . and now he was taking Jane with him!

As Annie digested Jane's news, she realized that she was sacrificing more than just her money for missions. Now she knew firsthand what it was to send a loved one onto the missions field. And because of Jane's leaving,

Annie had an even more personal connection to the work of missions her mother was always talking about.

When the Woman's Mission to Woman Society heard the news, the members were happy China was gaining a missionary but . . . what a shame they were losing her as the society recording secretary.

Eutaw Place Baptist Church planned a dedication and prayer service on April 17 for the Graveses and six other missionaries bound for China.

"Now, who are these other missionaries besides the Graveses?" a church member asked.

"Dr. and Mrs. Jesse B. Hartwell, Mrs. and Mrs. Nicholas B. Williams, and two single ladies, one of whom is Mrs. Williams's sister." This announcement caused a stir among the mission society members. They knew letters had been flowing from Martha Foster Crawford, a North China missionary, to Corinthia Williams, urging the Foreign Mission Society to push for appointment of single women missionaries. Mrs. Crawford desperately needed single women who could help assist her in evangelizing Chinese women.

"Why, the Foreign Mission Board has not seen fit to appoint single women missionaries for several years. Secretary Taylor did not seem to think highly of women missionaries or women's mission societies."

"It is said the new corresponding secretary is a great supporter of woman's work in missions. It is because of him, apparently, that the young single women are being appointed."

"Let us thank God!" a member stated. "What is this wonderful gentleman like?"

"I've heard Mr. Tupper is wealthy, has an aristocratic upbringing, and is quite the diplomat, but a visionary as well. The Board is blessed to have him."

The women allowed this information to soak in. They were too well bred to put in words what they all knew.

Mr. James Taylor, the former Foreign Mission Board corresponding secretary, had been decidedly against working with the women's societies, although he had asked for their money. Then, in October 1871, Woman's Mission to Woman had been reorganized to make it an all-Baptist group which was eager to support the Foreign Mission Board. At almost the same time Mr. Taylor suddenly died and Henry A. Tupper had taken his place. He had made working with the women's societies a top priority. With this newfound cooperation, the women were energized and funds were once again flowing to the Board for mission support.

"Well, who is the other single woman missionary besides Miss Whilden?" the questioner persisted.

"Some young girl named Edmonia Moon," came the answer. "Apparently she is paying her own travel expenses. She was just appointed on the ninth of this month."

The service was a moving time of prayer as the church sent out the missionaries, some new, some returning. Edmonia, whose nickname, it turned out, was Eddie, struck people as a young woman of strong intellect, with a great deal of energy and spirit.

As the congregation gathered for the service, Mrs. Graves entered with a visitor.

"I should like to introduce Mr. Hartwell's sister, Ellen Edwards. I invited her to Baltimore. She has traveled all the way from South Carolina," announced Mrs. Graves to some of the mission society members. Mrs. Edwards was greeted. Excitedly, she showed the women a little garnet-colored box with gold lettering. On the sides were printed Bible verses, the most conspicuous one being "To give light to them that sit in darkness." It also said, "Woman's Gospel Mission to Woman in Foreign Lands."

"Mrs. Graves has been introducing me to the idea of mite boxes," she explained. "I shall take several home to my church and encourage the women to set aside money for missions each week."

Two of the mission society members discussed the service after the missionaries had left for the train station.

"Oh, how we shall miss Jane! And that Eddie Moon is certainly a brave thing, isn't she, to go off to China so suddenly. Quite romantic—almost dashing, wouldn't you say?"

"Yeeesss," her friend answered slowly. "But still . . .," she hesitated, then plunged on. "Did she seem a little high-strung to you?"

Meanwhile, back in South Carolina, Ellen Edwards was showing the mite boxes to the women in her church. The women were to save at least 2 cents a week for missions—at one time it would not have seemed like such a great amount. With destruction from the war and the punishment that Reconstruction brought, however, 2 cents really did seem like "all their living."

"Will you try?" Ellen asked. "The missionaries—my brother included—are depending on us."

"Yes," the women all agreed. Christian teaching and the Civil War years had ingrained self-sacrifice into their characters. They would try. One of those who took a mite box was a gentle woman who looked rather like a prim schoolmarm. Ellen smiled over the mite box at her friend.

"Thank you, Mattie," she said to Martha McIntosh.

1873

"Let me guess—another trip to the Home?" a dapper young man said to Annie as she swept out the front door of her house. He had been passing by but stopped when she came out. He noticed she was carrying her usual Sunday afternoon tools—a sack of hard candy and her well-studied Bible. At that moment some of the young people from the church came up to join her.

"The Home of the Friendless has a friend in Miss Annie," one of them said. Silently, Annie thought of how giving a $5.00 donation to the home had put her on the board of managers, along with Mamie and Aunt Ann.

Well, she was glad it had worked out so. There were 100 orphans in the home, and they needed her Sunday afternoon Bible lesson.

"You know the Home means a great deal to me," she said to her friend.

"Yes, and sometime I shall come and help you with your good works. Perhaps at the big Christmas celebration," he replied.

Her dark eyes locked on his. "I shall hold you to that. Never tell me you are willing to work unless you really mean it!"

1878

Word rocketed around the church and neighborhood—Eutaw Place had formed a home and foreign missions committee with seven members, and a woman was asked to serve on it. Of course, it was generally agreed that sweet Alice Armstrong, with her bright mind and devotion to missions, was an asset to the committee. She was certainly following in her mother's footsteps of missions involvement. And Annie was no slouch herself. Though she lacked her sister's gentle nature, everyone knew that when the doors of Eutaw Place were open for services, Annie Armstrong would be there, sitting in the fifth pew with her mother and sister.

"But she doesn't seem as devoted to missions as Alice and Mary," a church member gossiped in the hall one Sunday morning.

"Yes, but she works so hard. Just look how she dotes on those children," came the answer. "She's been the Infant Class teacher for seven years now." And at that moment the six-foot-tall young woman came down the hallway, towering over her Primary Sunday School Class pupils.

"We've been invited to Miss Annie's house!" one excited child announced, but was quickly shushed by Miss Annie, who expected proper behavior in the church halls.

"Another tea party?" a teacher asked.

"You know how I like to entertain my little people with cups and saucers," Annie said with a smile and kept on going.

"I can't believe she has all those children come to her home. Whatever for?" the gossipy lady said disapprovingly after Annie and her flock had passed.

"Annie says it's the best way for her to get to know the children, and they enjoy it so," the teacher explained. "Alice serves the refreshments and Annie . . .," the woman paused to swallow her mirth, "Annie sits in the floor and plays jacks with them!"

"What foolishness. Children should be seen and not heard," the lady grumbled.

Annie's fellow teacher gave her a long look. With a little smile she quietly said, "I wouldn't say that to Annie if I were you."

1880

The members of the Woman's Baptist Foreign Mission Society sat quietly at their annual meeting, giving their full attention to the speaker. Corinthia Williams had invited Mrs. A. S. Quinton of Philadelphia to tell them about home missions, especially the conditions and needs of the Indians who had been forced onto reservations. As secretary of the National Indian Association, Mrs. Quinton spoke knowledgeably and movingly about the plight of tribes who had been torn from their ancestral lands. She painted a haunting picture of the Indians' destitution.

Annie absorbed every word the speaker uttered. Her mind soaked in the facts, but her heart ached with the awareness this knowledge brought. This woman wasn't talking about somewhere across the sea. These were people who were suffering in body and spirit right here in her homeland! The immigrants that flooded Baltimore, the orphans, the people in the Bay View Asylum—they had the ministry of many churches. Who did the Indians have to befriend them? Frontier churches were small and struggling. They could not do the work alone.

Later, Annie ignored the worries voiced by some society members that a concern for home missions would water down their foreign missions work. If God gave the work, God would supply the resources. Other women agreed with Annie. She and Corinthia led Eutaw Place and First Baptist Church to organize home mission societies.

1881

More than once people whispered to each other, "Do you think those girls will *ever* get married?" At 31 years of age, Annie was no longer a girl, and certainly seemed too busy doing a million other things to be spending any time husband hunting. There was her beloved Sunday School class, the young convert's committee, the committee on the poor, the orphans home, the Bay View Mission, and, finally, the missions committee. And when she wasn't involved in church and civic work, she and Alice were going to meetings in Chautauqua by the Lake in west New York.

"What do the ladies do at that Chautauqua doins'?" one family servant asked another as they packed Annie and Alice's belongings for another summer trip.

"Oh, it's a very improving thing. Miss Annie says they have classes. People lecture on things and they learn, and there are musicals. They both do a great deal of reading for it, from what I understand," the other servant replied as she neatly folded stockings and petticoats.

"Well, it's all the rage, I know, but it seems like an awful lot of mental exertion," the first servant observed. Her partner threw back her head and laughed.

"I think that's one reason they like it!"

And then there was Annie's friendship with Anne Luther Bagby.

The Bagbys, Anne and her husband, William, had left Texas on their way to the missions field of Brazil. After a visit with Mr. Tupper at the Foreign Mission Board (now International Mission Board), they went on to Maryland. They would leave from Baltimore's bustling port in January on a ship which just happened to be owned by the Leverings. The *Yamoyden* was a 483-ton sailing vessel used to export flour and import coffee through Baltimore's busy harbor. But they had some time before the ship sailed.

"Let's visit Eutaw Place," the Bagbys suggested to each other. They went to a night service and William spoke briefly about their work in Brazil. Dr. Rosewell Graves was there, back from China, and he spoke on Asian missions. Eutaw Place embraced the Bagbys. Annie and Anne met, and a lifelong friendship was born. Now Annie had a connection to both China and Brazil.

One of her China connections, Dr. Jesse B. Hartwell, had returned to Baltimore that same year. He and his wife had been among the missionaries in the dedication service in 1872. He had actually served in China since 1858; the wife who had been at his side in 1872, Julia, was the second Mrs. Hartwell. She fell ill on the trip to China and never really recovered. The couple had been seen in Baltimore in 1876, when Julia came to the city for medical treatment, her ill health having forced them to leave China the year before. In 1879 the Hartwells were appointed to work with the Chinese in California. Sadly, Julia caught a terrible cold on the way to her new missions field and died.

The people of Eutaw Place knew the missionary's story and were happy to see him that summer as he visited with friends in Baltimore. It was understood, though not openly discussed, that the Home Mission Board (now

North American Mission Board) had given him a leave of absence to come east and, as it was politely put, "accomplish the object of his visit." Obviously, everyone saw, the object of his visit was to find a third Mrs. Hartwell, who would be a mother to his children and fellow worker when he returned to China, which he longed to do.

"Now, you don't know that," cautioned one member of the congregation, seeking to put down gossip when the subject was mentioned.

"If he's not looking for a wife, why did the Home Mission Board authorize travel expenses back to California for him and *a wife?*" retorted another church member triumphantly.

"Oh, well, that puts a different aspect on it, doesn't it?"

Now the question of why Hartwell was in Baltimore had been settled, but the burning question was who would he choose as his new bride? There were several excellent young Christian women in the vicinity, including a certain tall, severe lady who had just turned 31 that summer. Certainly, she was 15 years younger that Hartwell, but Annie's mother had been 18 years younger than her father, so what of it? And Annie loved children so. Had she set her cap for him?

The speculation was quashed later when Hartwell married not Annie, but another Norris daughter—Jane's sister Charlotte. She was a member of Eutaw Place and a friend of Annie's. The couple wed in August. Some people speculated Annie had "given Mr. Hartwell the mitten," meaning she rejected him. Others thought he had never pursued her. Those who watched for signs of jealousy or disappointment in Annie saw only her concern for the family, especially the Hartwell children, as she faithfully corresponded with Charlotte through the coming years.

"Well, if she's crushed, she's doing a fine job of hiding it," the curious in the church finally had to concede as Annie marched from one task to another. One task dear to her heart was the Bay View Mission, a ministry to the Bay View Asylum, Baltimore's poorhouse. Annie started the mission and served as its president for many years. Through service to the mission she learned about fundraising as she worked with the Women's Christian Temperance Union, the Enoch Pratt Library, Baptist women, and nondenominational organizations. Annie was relentless in getting help of all kinds for the 2,500 people admitted annually to the asylum.

"It is the largest opportunity, I expect, in the city of Baltimore that one can have to reach the unsaved in one day, outside of the jail or penitentiary," she explained. Most of the people at the asylum were between the ages of 20 and 50, normally the prime of adult life; but mental illness, disease, and alcoholism had blighted the promise and strength that should have been theirs.

"How can she stand to even go to that place?" a neighbor asked. "A well-bred young lady among all those degenerates."

"They are not degenerates!" the unlucky speaker turned to see Annie behind her. "They are poor unfortunates and we could just as easily be in their place," she said, her voice almost breaking with compassion on the words *poor unfortunates*. The speaker was just giving voice to what most decent people thought of the poor, the ill, and addicted. Annie thought otherwise, and was not afraid to say so.

As a matter of fact, more and more people realized, Annie was not afraid of much of anything. Since it appeared she might not marry, perhaps she would follow in her father's footsteps and go into business. Perhaps she would join such women as Eddie and Lottie Moon on the missions field. There was just no telling what that Armstrong woman would do.

3

The Woman's Baptist Home Mission Society of Maryland

Wetumka, Creek Nation, Indian Territory, Spring 1882

At the Levering Manual Labor School, a worried school administrator sat hunched over a desk, writing furiously. Through the window drifted the voices of Indian children at play. It was the needs of those children that prompted the superintendent to write a letter of appeal to the Baptist women of Eutaw Place and First Church in Baltimore.

The letter spelled out the problem facing the six-month-old school. The school had been depending on a sum of money promised by the Indian government. That money had not been paid. The ladies of Eutaw Place had already clothed 20 students, but . . . 240 boys and girls needed summer suits. Could they please find some way to help?

Baltimore, Late Spring 1882

When the letter arrived it electrified the Home Mission Society. "Where are we going to get 240 children's suits?" the members asked each other. True, they had a special bond to the school because it had been made possible by a $2,500 legacy that Annie's uncle, Eugene Levering Sr., had left the Home Mission Board. True, they had clothed children before, but this project was going to require cooperation.

The Home Mission Society of First Baptist Church had also received a plea from the superintendent. First Church, while willing to help, also owned that 240 suits was beyond their reach. The two societies formed a committee to approach their sister churches, black and white, with the request.

"Who would have thought summer suits for children would have caused this excitement?" The women in the church lecture hall marveled at the number of suits that were being folded and packed into shipping barrels.

"Churches have given money and suits," another mission society member said. "I wonder just how many?"

"Eight white churches and six black churches responded," said the first woman as she worked. "And I hear that new home mission societies are being formed so the women can continue the work. God has truly blessed our willingness with opportunity."

"Willingness is all well and good," said her friend. "But I hope there's somebody nearby that knows how to keep all these efforts working smoothly. Let us pray God blesses us with a leader along with all this wonderful opportunity!"

The two women looked up then to see a tall woman stride past, jotting something down in a small black notebook as she walked. She had been everywhere at once it seemed, encouraging the women while directing them to do things in a precise, orderly way. For some reason upon seeing her the two women felt a sudden urge to return to their work.

"There goes Annie Armstrong," remarked the first woman as she went back to packing suits.

May 6, 1882

Amid the soft rustling of silk and woolen skirts, the representatives of the women's home mission societies of Baltimore took their seats in Eutaw Place for their organizational meeting. After the success of the school summer suit project, Annie and other women had seen it was time for more organization among the growing societies. Today, they would form a central committee to function as the state organization for women's home mission societies throughout Maryland.

Each point of business was decided in turn. What would they call this central committee? The Woman's Baptist Home Mission Society of Maryland. What was its objective? To cooperate with the Home Mission Board and induce a spirit of united work among the women of all the churches. What was its growth goal? To have an auxiliary in every church. What was its organizational structure? The president of each society would be a vice-president of the general society, and the general society would receive contributions from the churches.

Who would be its president? Annie Armstrong. Her leadership and organizational abilities, her energy, and her passion for missions made her the obvious choice.

The superintendent of the Levering Manual Labor School rejoiced that not only did students receive the summer suits but the school remained a top project of the Baltimore women. Annie had not forgotten Mrs. Quinton's report about the needs on the reservations. Other women shared her excitement. At the end of the first year of the society's operation, 11 churches—black, white, city, and country—had given almost $530 in clothes or money to the school. Yet so much more lay waiting to be done, and Annie knew who could help her find the right direction for the committee to take. She sat down and composed a letter to Isaac Taylor Tichenor, the new corresponding secretary of the Home Mission Board (now North American Mission Board).

But would he answer? She wondered. While Henry Tupper had been busy encouraging women's support of the Foreign Mission Board, the Home Mission Board had barely acknowledged their existence, much less asked for very much help. True, Tichenor had encouraged the women with the Levering School in Indian Territory. But with only 31 out of 500 church women's mission societies contributing to home missions, it seemed the brethren might not want them.

One day when she came home the servant girl met her with the mail, including a letter from Atlanta. When Annie saw who it was from, she did not even wait to take off her hat before opening it. Getting a letter was not unusual for Annie, but this one was a reply from Mr. Tichenor. She knew that as the new corresponding secretary for the Home Mission Board, he had great responsibility. At the Southern Baptist Convention that year, things had come to such a pass that the delegates had been ready to disband the Home Mission Board. Tichenor agreed to leave the presidency of Auburn University and head the Board. Now the Home Mission Board not only had a new corresponding secretary but a new location. It was moved out of hard-to-reach Marion, Alabama, and into the New South city of Atlanta. Yet with all that to deal with, he had answered her.

As she tore into the letter she again hoped he had plenty of ideas and suggestions, for she did not want to do anything contrary to the Home Mission Board's wishes. But . . . there was so much the society could do to help the cause of missions! She just knew it.

Waco, Texas, 1883

While the men met for the Southern Baptist Convention, women gathered for their own meeting, as they had for several years. Travel was so difficult, it could not be expected for many of their eastern sisters to attend. Also, travel and lodging costs made women an unnecessary Convention expense. The Texas women, however, sent the invitation out far and wide to their Baptist sisters. A record number of delegates showed up in Waco, and 700 Baptist women, all of whom were met with a Texas-sized welcome. While the men had to sleep on cots in churches, the ladies were boarded in private homes. Cake, chicken, ham, pie, and bread rolled into town by the wagonload.

Corinthia Williams's husband, John, gave the women's report at the Convention and emphasized the good work the women were doing. Meanwhile, the women were having their own meeting at the Methodist church.

"Is that who I think it is?" one delegate asked another as a striking looking woman with black hair and eyes took her place as presider.

"Yes! It's Sallie Rochester Ford. Oh, isn't she wonderful? Such a brave woman to speak and pray in public."

"I wish I'd known she was presiding. I just love her novel *Grace Truman*. I would have asked her to sign it!" the first woman responded.

Her neighbor's reply was stopped by the opening hymn. Hundreds of women's voices sang out "Nearer My God to Thee." Sallie's husband read the Scriptures, and Sallie introduced Martha Crawford, home from China on a much-needed furlough (now stateside assignment). A ripple of unease ran through the room when some women realized the men would stay to hear Mrs. Crawford. Those who didn't realize it were made aware of it when Mr. J. A. Hackett of Louisiana rose and said in his folksy way, "Let every one keep quiet [*sic*] now; this is the opportunity of our lives."

Martha Crawford, in her gentle way, put everyone at ease. This wouldn't be a speech or a sermon, just a missionary speaking of China in a general way and answering some questions. She talked and answered questions for some time.

The next day John Williams encouraged the women to organize, and then Mrs. Crawford spoke again. She was riveting. The women were so excited they had an extra meeting at a hotel to discuss matters more.

The delegates left Waco stuffed with good food and more energized for missions than ever. The next year, they understood, the Convention would take place on the coast; the Baptists there could have a better opportunity to attend. The women who could travel looked forward to meeting in Baltimore, though surely the women there could not offer better hospitality than the women of Waco had shown.

1884

"Why does the Home Mission Society not help host the women's meeting during the Convention?" asked Mary Armstrong. She said it by way of suggestion, not criticism, and her daughter took up the idea immediately. The Maryland Foreign Mission Society, which was planning the meeting, had invited women from each missionary society in the South. The meeting would be held, however, not at a Baptist church, but at Westminster Presbyterian Church on May 8.

The meeting was wonderful. Annie met other state missions leaders. She heard Adele Fielde, a Baptist Missionary Union missionary to China. Her thoughts drifted momentarily to Charlotte and Jane, who had gone to China. Then her attention returned to the meeting as she was urged to subscribe to the Kentucky women's missionary paper, the *Heathen Helper*. The women finished the meeting in agreement that they would meet each year during the Convention. The women in whose state the Convention was held would be in charge of the meeting.

Though busy with the women's meeting, Annie was not oblivious to the actual Convention itself. She couldn't be, with what her cousin Joshua Levering had planned. Her stalwart cousin had dared offer a resolution that the Home Mission Board appoint a woman to oversee the women's work for home missions. The woman would visit cities to organize mission societies, give and collect information, and strengthen the work of women as they strengthened missions.

When word of the resolution reached the women, they were riveted. They took note of all the debate, and some women sat in on the Convention sessions as visitors. After lunch the messengers met to discuss the resolution. The men who opposed the resolution raged. J. William Jones, a Confederate veteran and much respected, denounced the idea. "It is the entering wedge of Woman's Rights! Our Southern ladies do not want to do such work."

Other men warned of the possibility that the women would form their own mission board and criticized women speaking in public. Another messenger rose. "A woman might just as well be employed to collect and disseminate information about colored people as do this kind of work," he sneered. He looked around, certain he had hit upon the ultimate insult. But he had not delivered the final blow after all.

A young man named J. B. Gambrell shot back, "The Convention is just being a bunch of old fogies." The women grew nervous as the men on the floor grew angrier. If name calling had started, could fisticuffs and challenges to duel be far behind?

Apparently John Williams thought so. He quickly moved that the proposal be referred to the Home Mission Board, where no doubt a committee could study it.

"I wonder if Annie Armstrong put her cousin up to making that resolution," one messenger speculated. The messengers were never to know. Joshua and Annie kept their own counsel on whether the two had discussed his plans.

Later, when other women asked what had become of Joshua's resolution, they were told it had been sent to the Home Mission Board for discussion. "That means it's dead," muttered one woman. With sinking hearts, the other women admitted she was right.

Augusta, Georgia, 1885

The Southern Baptist Convention was meeting once again, and tension was high. The women had heard that Dr. Tupper was going to present in his report for the Foreign Mission Board a daring idea—that the women's central committees be considered a part of the SBC and allow them to appoint delegates. As if this were not enough excitement, the Baptists of Arkansas had sent two women as duly accredited messengers. One was Mary Oldham Eagle, who just happened to be married to the president of the Arkansas State Convention. She herself was the president of the Arkansas women. The other was Margaretta Dudley, secretary of the women's central committee and a pastor's wife. Female visitors and male messengers watched the drama unfold on the Convention floor. Would the women be seated?

J. William Jones protested. He showed the tenacious fighting streak that had probably kept him alive through the Civil War two decades earlier. A committee of five was called. Since three men were sympathetic to the women and were related to many of the women leaders, the majority report approved seating them as messengers. "The Constitution does not prohibit women serving as messengers," they stated.

"We wish to submit a minority report," Jones snapped, speaking for himself and the other member. "The founders of the Southern Baptist Convention never envisioned women wanting to be messengers, or they would have written the rules more carefully. Besides," the old warrior added, "our Southern women did not desire to be members of the Convention."

Eagle and Dudley looked at each other. In the balcony, women spectators rolled their eyes. The messengers were beginning to think the room was exceedingly warm, and not just from the Georgia sunshine.

The insults continued to fly. J. B. Hawthorne, who should have known better since his wife had once headed the Alabama Central Committee, endeared himself to J. William Jones when he sputtered, "I love the women but dread them more. If ladies are admitted as delegates, they will be qualified for any office." Hawthorne painted the picture of the presidency of the Southern Baptist Convention going to a woman because no decent man would want it anymore. And he finished with the battle cry, "Our Southern women do not want it."

Not only were the women messengers excluded from the Convention, the constitution was changed so that the neutral word *messenger* was expunged and the word *brethren* fixed in its place. That would show those women and the men who dared provoke them!

Then Henry Tupper made his report, and the men tore apart his proposal. Not only would the SBC not recognize the women's committees, the sponsorship of those committees would go to the state Baptist conventions. Ever the gentle servant of the Convention, Tupper tried to express himself in courteous terms throughout the whole awful discussion, but he sat down feeling terrible.

"Poor Dr. Tupper," the sympathetic messengers murmured among themselves. "He sought to make things better for the ladies, and now it's only worse." The other messengers congratulated each other on their handling of both situations. The women were discouraged, some in despair, some just plain angry. Why continue to try to work with those who did not even want them around? they asked each other.

There *were* men who wanted them around, however, and appreciated the work the women did. Dr. Tupper gave what he hoped were words of encouragement to his Christian sisters.

"Refuse to be discouraged by opposition. No good thing has ever failed to arouse opposition. . . . Make no resistance, keep on the even tenor of your way, and by gentleness and kindness disarm criticism." After this comforting message, Tupper tried to reason with the brethren who felt threatened by women serving God.

"Whatever the danger that the mission work, as between men and women, may grow out of proportion—and this danger has been fully recognized—yet, so long as their combined effort falls immeasurably short of the world's necessities, it is wiser to stimulate the men than to restrain the women. If one sex neglects our Lord's Great Commission, the other should not be compelled to do the same."

The men were unmoved.

1886

"Alice, look. What a rich opportunity!" Alice knew her sister was not speaking about monetary riches, for Annie did not get that excited about money.

"What opportunity? An opportunity to do more work, no doubt?" Alice was only teasing. If Annie thought something was worthwhile, Alice usually did, too.

"The editors of the *Baltimore Baptist* have said if the home and foreign mission societies will try to encourage subscriptions, the editors will give the societies a regular column in the paper. We can take turns with the foreign mission society. And *you* can be the editor for the home missions column!"

Alice couldn't refuse. It was indeed too rich an opportunity for spreading missions information. And while Annie was the great organizer, she was better suited to serving the Lord with her pen. Also, Alice admitted to herself, it was a way, not to boast of their work, certainly, but to let skeptical men and apathetic women see what they were doing for the cause of missions. The sisters, though not present at the Augusta fiasco, had heard plenty about it, and were determined to continue the fight.

Around the same time Alice was beginning her stint as a newspaper columnist, Annie became involved in her biggest project yet. The Maryland Baptist Union Association decided at their October meeting to establish a missionary library and reading room in Baltimore. If they were to promote missions, there must be better knowledge and understanding of missions. Better and more accessible literature was one way to increase that knowledge.

The committee was formed: Baltimore pastors A. C. Dixon, A. J. Rowland, and (Annie's pastor) F. M. Ellis would carry out the recommendation. To the women's amazement, their foreign and home mission societies were asked to each contribute a member to the committee.

With winter coming soon and making travel difficult, Annie and another woman quickly set out for Philadelphia. There they studied the work of the Baptist Women's Missionary Bureau, which had just begun operating that year, and the Presbyterian Mission Rooms, which had been started earlier. The women learned much, but decided on a bigger project than either of those mission rooms. They envisioned reading rooms, a library, even a catalog from which Baptists could order a variety of missions literature. Patrons would have access not only to Baptist literature but the best missions resources of many denominations. Since so few people ever traveled out West or abroad, they would have curios from other lands to spark the interest of visitors to the rooms. It would be the closest many people ever got, Annie realized, to the fields where the missionaries served.

Winter 1887

In January, Annie and the committee of women from the mission societies met to plan the reading rooms. It was a daunting task, but Annie was ready. She had already been part of a committee that furnished Eutaw Place. The business part of running the rooms did not bother her; business was in her blood.

As the women talked, it became obvious that it would be best for the men to raise money for expenses and act as an advisory committee. The women would furnish the rooms and run them. Now that the organization had been planned, a new committee was needed, one to actually run what they had named the Maryland Mission Rooms. Now, all they had to do was actually find a location, gather materials, enlist volunteers, and promote the reading rooms.

As the days passed, the women looked for space and let it be known they were shopping around. Henry Marvin Wharton, publisher of the *Baltimore Baptist*, came to their aid.

"Ladies, I would like to offer the upper room at the Wharton and Barron Publishing Company for the use of the Maryland Mission Rooms." Then he added the magic words, "Rent free."

Eagerly, the women went over to check out their new rooms. Their glee faded away when they saw the location, or rather, how they were supposed to reach the new location. To get to the upper room, one had to climb a ladder which went straight up on the outside of the building. The women looked at each other and then down in dismay at their long dresses and high-top shoes.

"No decent woman is going to be caught climbing up and down that ladder!" one woman cried.

"If she did, she'd likely break her neck tripping over the hem of her skirt," groaned another. The women were in a quandary. How to bring this up in a modest way to generous Dr. Wharton? A lady did not even refer to a chair as having legs, much less confess to having any of her own. They could not possibly tell Dr. Wharton they were afraid if they climbed the steep ladder they would either break their heretofore unmentionable legs or have unchivalrous men sneaking a peek at their petticoats.

As embarrassing as it was, they explained their concerns to Dr. Wharton, who understood completely.

"May I offer a solution, ladies?" he asked.

"Please do," the committee responded.

"I shall hold a lecture. You shall sell tickets to the lecture, and use the money to build a stairway to provide adequate access to your reading rooms."

Annie and the other women were delighted with the suggestion. Dr. Wharton was a famous speaker and there would be no problem selling tickets to any lecture he gave. Sure enough, a decent stairway was built on the outside wall of the publishing house, leading to the upper rooms.

Annie passed the winter collecting missions periodicals and books, finding tracts and leaflets to sell, printing the catalog, and buying furniture. The women gathered curios to display. Volunteers were enlisted to keep the rooms open for visitors and fill catalog orders. The Maryland Mission Rooms opened in March. They caught on immediately.

As summer came on, a problem arose of how to run the mission rooms when volunteers went out of town for the summer. Annie, who chaired the quarterly Executive Committee meetings in addition to all her other work, offered to take up the slack. There was only one problem. Annie, too, was supposed to leave town and vacation in Virginia with some of her family. She resisted, but Mary and Alice, supported by Mamie, Eugene, and Joshua, insisted.

"You need a change. It's a well-known fact that breathing all this city air will sap your health" was the way their argument ran. Annie surrendered. She could stand against almost anything except the loving pressure of her family.

But Annie would not go without a fall-back plan. When a mission room volunteer said, "How will you manage the work while your family is in Virginia?" Annie announced she was taking the work with her.

And she did exactly that. While she couldn't put the whole reading room in her valise, she did take the items the committee was having published.

When they arrived in Virginia, Annie had to admit, it was lovely. Their vacation spot was in the mountains, a place of fresh air, silence, and beautiful vistas. She was spared the painful sights and sounds of the city streets: little waifs selling matches, their age and gender obscured under layers of dirt and rags; peddlers of all kinds yelling out their services or wares; and occasionally, in a bad section of town, women who appeared to be not overly virtuous. Not all of Baltimore was like McCulloh Street.

One day while Annie and Alice were out enjoying themselves, a gentleman approached them and asked to make their acquaintance.

"I am Mr. Dickinson, editor of the *Religious Herald* of Virginia," he announced. The sisters were delighted to meet him, and he found them charming. He liked both sisters, but Alice's writing ability impressed him.

"Could I impose on you, Miss Alice, to write a column on the women's issue for the paper?" he asked one day. Alice knew exactly what women's issue he meant—the struggle to organize the societies that supported the mission boards. She accepted, with the stipulation that she write under a pen name.

Annie beamed at the idea of Alice's words appearing in the influential Baptist newspaper. Meanwhile, she was stealing every moment she could from the vacation to work on the publications for the mission rooms. In addition to two leaflets and two editions of quarterly programs, the committee planned to issue a prayer card. The prayer card was really a four-page card featuring a missions field for each month with statistics and an inspiring Scripture passage. Later the committee would add supplemental leaflets based on the card outline. Annie made sure to enlist the best Southern Baptist leaders to provide the content. She believed in seeking out only the finest quality in everything, including writers.

Vacation ended and the Armstrongs returned to Baltimore, with their lungs full of fresh air and a rosy glow to their faces. October came around again. It had been just one short year since the idea of the mission rooms had even been brought up. Now it was time for the Maryland Baptist Union Association annual meeting. The delegates were treated to the first report about the project. The mission rooms had the start of a very good library. It had filled orders from 31 states and territories and Canada. The leaflets and prayer card had been published, and more were planned.

Annie was becoming more well known in Baptist circles. She was "indefatigable," everyone agreed. And with the mission rooms, her role as the president of the Woman's Baptist Home Mission Society, her Sunday School class, the Bay View Mission, family, and committee work, she had her hands full. Yes, friends and neighbors told each other, even Miss Annie could not take on one more job. But Annie wasn't so sure.

4
Founding of WMU

Louisville, Kentucky, May 6, 1887

While the men convened for the Southern Baptist Convention, 300 women gathered at Broadway Methodist Church. Sallie Rochester Ford presided for the fourth time. Anne Bagby, home from Brazil, spoke to the women. Then the states gave their reports. Since Maryland had two central committees, one for home missions and one for foreign, there were two delegates. Annie spoke for home missions, and Mrs. James Pollard represented the Foreign Mission Society. When it was time for Maryland's report, Annie noted among her comments that the Woman's Home Mission Society of Maryland had raised $2,415.48.

But underneath all the activity, the question of organization simmered. Mrs. G. A. Gammage of St. Louis presented a paper suggesting the appointment of an advisory board to be in charge of the annual meetings and to communicate with the state central committees. In addition to the paper, the women had debated the merits of better organization, better ways of distributing missions information, and, as always, ideas for more systematic giving. The women knew systematic giving meant better giving.

Anticipation was high among the 300 women. Would this be the year they organized, bringing each state central committee together in a Convention-wide effort? Had it been up to Annie, the answer would have been yes. Instead, it was a sorrowful no.

"We have not the authority to organize," some of the women told those in favor of immediate organization. They realized they were not duly appointed delegates. No one had given them the power to speak for their respective states. What would they do?

In the confusion a dignified woman stepped forward and offered a resolution. Annie Armstrong, though eager, wanted everything to be done properly, even if that meant taking extra time. She suggested that each state appoint three delegates to meet during next year's Convention and "to decide upon the advisability of organizing a general committee; and if so, to provide for it's operation." The women found this to be an excellent plan.

Some of the brethren, however, did not. Dr. Tupper, with all his talent, had not been able to sway everyone to his way of thinking. Preachers used their pulpits and newspaper editors used their pages as avenues for working against the organizing of women.

"I don't understand," said one of the Armstrong family friends. "What are they afraid of? What do they think Annie, Alice, and the others are trying to do?"

"There is great change happening everywhere," Mary explained. "Some women are agitating to go outside their appointed sphere. Some even want to vote. A few of the brethren think next we will be wanting to preach and teach men. Most of the men fear that we will ultimately take money away from the boards by appointing our own missionaries. But we have no desire to do that. We simply wish to help the boards and the missionaries. Millions are dying without hearing of the Savior!"

"With the resistance, it looks as if organization is doomed," the friend said helpfully.

While these kinds of conversations were going on, an article on the topic appeared in the *Religious Herald*. Men read it, some at their own choosing, some at the urging of their wives and mothers. The writer, Ruth Alleyn, said, "There is a sound of shaking in the tops of the trees and we feel abundantly persuaded that the wind which is stirring the peaceful commotion is none other than the spirit of the living God."

"What do you think of the article, Annie?" a mission society member asked. "This Ruth Alleyn certainly knows how to make a point, doesn't she?" Annie looked at Alice. The sisters smiled at each other. Yes, Annie thought quite highly of Ruth Alleyn and her articles, especially since the gifted Ruth Alleyn was none other than her big sister Alice.

October 1887

At Louisville the women had agreed to Annie's proposal that each state central committee appoint three delegates to the 1888 meeting in Richmond, where the question of organization would again be discussed. It was understood these delegates would be empowered to express their states' wishes on the issue. Martha McIntosh had been named chairwoman of the committee to arrange the next meeting, though the Virginia women would be hosts. Within days of the Louisville meeting Martha had sent information to each state central committee and asked them to choose their delegates.

Now it was October and both the home and foreign missions central committees of Maryland needed to choose delegates. In a meeting of the Home Mission Society, Annie emphatically argued for organization. "It is a help to wider knowledge and better plans," she said. "I consider women's work to be a force fore-ordained of God." There was really no question who would be the society's delegate. It had to be Annie. The Home Mission Society communicated to the Foreign Mission Society that they would like Mrs. Pollard to be a joint delegate from both societies.

The Foreign Mission Society, however, had its own mind. After a long discussion, in which the society favored South Carolina as the location for the general committee, organization was approved and Mrs. A. J. Rowland, not Mrs. Pollard, was the delegate. Mrs. Pollard and Mrs. O. F. Gregory would be alternates.

As word spread through the Baptist grapevine, Annie and her co-workers discovered that other state central committees were having a harder time than they. North Carolina men were so afraid the women were breaking the bounds of propriety they had dissolved the committee altogether. It was a shame, for Mattie Heck of Raleigh could have made an outstanding leader. Virginia had also dissolved its central committee, and others were struggling. The women prayed for help and guidance, and help came from across the sea in China.

December 1887

"Annie, look at this letter from Miss Lottie Moon in the *Foreign Mission Journal*." Annie took the publication and read the letter, finding herself more inspired and determined at every word the China missionary wrote.

"Some years ago the Southern Methodist mission in China had run down to the lowest water-mark; the rising of the tide seems to have begun with the enlisting of the women of the church in the cause of missions. The previously unexampled increase in missionary zeal and activity in the Northern Presbyterian church is attributed to the same reason—the thorough awakening of the women of the church upon the subject of missions. In like manner, until the women of the Southern Baptist churches are thoroughly aroused, we shall continue to go on in our present 'hand to mouth' system. We shall continue to see mission stations so poorly manned that missionaries break down from overwork, loneliness, and isolation; we shall continue to see promising mission fields unentered and old stations languishing; and we shall continue to see other denominations no richer and no better educated than ours, outstripping us in the race."

Her eyes raced across the page and she found her heart stirred by these words: "I am convinced that one of the chief reasons our Southern Baptist women do so little is the lack of organization. Why should we not learn from these noble Methodist women, and instead of the paltry offerings we make, do something that will prove we are really in earnest in claiming to be the followers of Him Who 'though he was rich, for our sake became poor'?"

Like Annie, women across the Southern Baptist Convention read those words and were likewise stirred by them. Men who were in favor of women's work cheered the article; those who had been on the fence about the matter began to lean more on the side of organization. This was proof, the women told each other, proof that organization was needed and wanted! Surely the time was right.

Richmond, May 11–14, 1888

Annie looked out her bedroom window. It was a rainy Friday morning, but she was not one to let the weather dictate her plans, especially not today of all days. She set out to meet the other 31 delegates and hundreds of visitors gathering at Broad Street Methodist Church. The leaders of the meeting had spent all of Thursday in prayer, seeking God's will and guidance. As long as they were doing God's will, a way would be found for them. Annie had learned that truth at her mother's knee.

The Virginia women were in a quandary. They were to host the meeting, but the state convention had disbanded their central committee. Henry Tupper came to the rescue again and had the Foreign Mission Board take responsibility for the committee. Not only did he need the women's support, but also he had a fatherly interest in their success. His daughter Mary was committee secretary.

The meeting was held in a spacious ground-floor room in the church. There were well over 200 women in attendance, but Annie's main interest was in the 32 official delegates. These were women from 12 states. Alabama sent no delegates, but there were Alabama women there.

South Carolina had sent the woman who had accepted Ellen Edwards's mite box back in 1872, Martha McIntosh (Mattie to her friends). She had become a powerhouse for missions organization both in her home state and during the annual meetings. Though she and Annie were very different, Annie had grown to respect Martha for her devotion and wisdom. The respect was mutual. And they had something else in common. Like Annie, Martha depended on another woman to help her succeed. When she inherited the family estate, she found herself encumbered with running the mansion. Fanny Stout took her to live with her so that Martha could devote herself to missions without the distractions of keeping up a house.

Annie saw the presider, Anne Whitfield. She was married to Theodore Whitfield, a Virginia pastor and friend of missions. In their last pastorate, the young couple had organized the church women for missions, with Anne as president and her husband as secretary. Anne had not wanted the job of presiding, and she had not been their first choice. Sallie Rochester Ford had declined. After presiding four times, no one could say she had not done her duty. Mattie Heck of North Carolina also refused. She felt that being pregnant at age 46 was a good reason to stay close to home, but sent her daughter Fannie Exile Scudder Heck as an observer.

Annie noted that young Mrs. Whitfield looked nervous. That was not good. It had taken all the persuasive powers of the Virginia committee to get her to agree to lead the meeting in the first place.

But then Annie caught sight of her pastor, Dr. Ellis, and her optimism surged. He had been invited to conduct the morning's devotion. Annie knew he would do a wonderful job. Dr. Ellis was known for his oratory, and he had a charming way about him. It didn't hurt their cause, Annie knew, that Dr. Ellis was also highly popular at the Southern Baptist Convention now taking place.

As the women settled down and came to order, Dr. Ellis led the opening religious exercises. Then he got down to business. He spoke of not making difficulties appear larger than they actually were. He urged the women to realize the strength they possessed. He laughed at the idea the meeting was secretly a woman's rights rally.

"All fear ought to be put aside before the overmastering thought of divine . . . service," he preached. Annie and others who were ready for action hung on his every word. The handsome young preacher had to leave the meeting then, as it would have been highly inappropriate for a man to be in the audience while the women conducted business.

After he left, Jennie Hatcher, the president of the Virginia committee, greeted the women and introduced Anne Whitfield as presider. To Annie's relief, instead of following Ellis's lead and making a hasty run for the exit, Mrs. Whitfield accepted the responsibility. Agnes Osborne, the editor of Kentucky's *Heathen Helper*, had agreed to be secretary.

Fanny Stout then read her paper on the benefits of organizing for missions. Mrs. Whitfield called the roll of states to give their opinion about organizing. She called Maryland first. This was the moment Annie had been waiting for. She declared, "Maryland heartily approves of an organization." She then unleashed a torrent of facts and statistics to back up their desire to organize. Were the delegates aware that in 1887 Southern Baptist women gave $11,333 to foreign missions and $5,000 to home missions? Lest this sound impressive she went on to point out this was less than 3 cents per capita. Yet, thousands died daily without knowing the saving grace of Jesus.

To her delight, most of the delegates of other states agreed. Fannie Davis of Texas put their thoughts into words when she spoke up. "This movement is not for 'woman's rights,' though we have our rights, the highest of which is the right for service."

Mississippi, however, demurred. "Mississippi is not yet ready to commit to organization," the delegates said. Though not a delegate, Fannie Heck indicated that she knew North Carolina was not ready either.

Then the Virginia women really slowed down the process. They were not sure what action they should take.

"Virginia wishes to wait until the Convention has made its feelings known," the delegation announced.

Annie could not bear to see the momentum slowing. This went against everything in her character. Did these women not realize they must go forward? Why must they wait for the Convention to give its blessing? Had they forgotten already what Dr. Ellis had said? She spoke up, reminding the women that many key Southern Baptist men had already taken a stand on their behalf.

"The work and its attendant responsibilities are our own. The history of religious work has not shown that it could afford to wait for majorities," she said. Some of the women nodded, while others looked uncomfortable. The question arose, why not sack the program and get right to organizing?

Jennie Hatcher, however, was not easily intimidated. She had been one of Lottie Moon's peers in boarding school, and if she could live with someone as strong and determined as Lottie Moon, she could certainly stand up to Annie Armstrong.

"I deplore undue haste and urge a strict compliance with the program," she replied. Things were getting a bit testy, and it was still the first session.

"Then I suggest calling an extra meeting in which important concerns can be aired and addressed," Annie said, fearing she had pushed too hard. Then diplomatic Mrs. Pollard stepped in with a solution.

"The matter has been under consideration for a year," she reminded them in her gentle southern drawl. "Shall we go on with the program, while appointing one delegate from each state to draft a constitution this weekend? The committee can bring its report Monday." Her suggestion was approved. Martha McIntosh would chair the constitution committee and Annie would be the committee member representing Maryland. It just so happened that she and Mrs. Pollard had brought a constitution with them. Mrs. Pollard had the expertise of her lawyer husband, and Annie had Alice to help with the wording. This was the constitution the Home Mission Society had adopted a month earlier. Annie and Mrs. Pollard had secured the society's permission to take it to Richmond. Even with the Baltimore constitution, Annie and the others found themselves poring over the draft all weekend.

"Any constitution must withstand the scrutiny of the men," it was noted when they began. "Some will be looking for any reason to rip it apart. We must show that we can understand such matters from a legal and practical viewpoint."

"And we must reassure them we are not trying to set up our own mission board," another delegate pointed out.

"Then let us prayerfully set to work." And they did. Besides everything already discussed, the committee took into account the status of the present state central committees as well as the work of the societies. By Monday morning the committee was tired, but ready.

Meanwhile, Ellis was preaching a stewardship sermon on Friday night, and could only be gratified when he looked into the congregation and saw it was packed with the same women he had spoken to earlier that day.

Then, on Saturday during the Convention he looked up to the church balcony to see it overflowing with women. They had come to hear him deliver the report of the committee on Convention improvements. The report delved into such weighty matters as changes in the basis of representation, how the Convention should relate to the state, systematic giving, and women's work.

The harmlessly worded part about women's work was buried in the middle of the report. The committee recommended encouraging missionary circles and children's bands in all the churches and using established channels to send contributions to the mission boards. The boards would keep track of the women's contributions. The societies were invited to make reports annually to the mission boards. By dealing directly with the boards, the central committees would no longer be so completely under the thumb of hostile state conventions.

Ellis and others braced for the fierce debate they expected; it came, but not over the women's issue. Other parts were debated at length until the men got tired and wanted to be done with the whole thing. The whole report passed by a wide margin.

It was almost too good to be true, some of the men thought. They were brought down to earth by the comments of some men who could not let go of their fear of women organizing. One Kentucky messenger threatened the other messengers with Paul. "You can't overthrow Paul, and Paul said, 'If you vote for this organization, God only knows what the women will do. Nobody on the face of this earth will be able to manage them, and they will be in danger of wrecking the whole business.'" He did not say which version of the Scriptures he was quoting.

The Kentuckian and his warning did not sway the Convention. The report was good, it was voted on, and the messengers wanted to go to a reception at the governor's mansion, so that was that.

Monday morning was May 14, and missionary John Eager led the morning devotions to a crowd of enthusiastic delegates. The women felt the burden of What did the Convention think? had been lifted. As long as they sent their money, the Convention didn't care, they told each other. After the devotions the women belted out "Rock of Ages." Then Alice Armstrong presented her paper.

"I have titled this paper, 'Special Obligations of Woman to Spread the Gospel,'" she began, and launched into a powerful message. She had based her points on the Bible, using examples of women from the Scriptures. The women thrilled to Alice describing how "earnest, godly women with willing hearts, ready hands and fire-crowned tongues, gave of their substance, their labor and their consecrated words for the cause of God and the good of their fellows." The Christian woman of America should compare her privileges with her degraded, hopeless sisters both at home and abroad. Woman should take the tender heart and keen sensibilities with which she had been endowed by God and use her abilities to spread the gospel. Together, Baptist women could be a power for good.

She reminded the delegates that "tiresome halting or painful wavering is alike needless. God's word comes to us in plain command and instructive example." When Alice knew she had the women hanging on her every word, she reached the crescendo of her argument. At this point, when women knew their obligation and knew they needed each other to act effectively, an organization—working through the churches—would stimulate, sustain, and perfect their efforts. It was not a matter of whether they were obligated to spread the gospel, but *how*.

When Alice finished it was time for the constitutional committee to report. "Before we begin, let us pray for guidance," Martha McIntosh intoned. After the prayer, the constitution was read aloud. Like the United States Constitution, it had a preamble. It began:

"We, the women of the churches connected with the Southern Baptist Convention, desirous of stimulating the missionary spirit and the grace of giving among the women and children of the churches, and aiding in collecting funds for missionary purposes, to be disbursed by the Boards of the Southern Baptist Convention, and disclaiming all intention of independent action, organize . . ."

The chairwoman put the delegates on notice there would be a roll call of the states for the official organization vote.

"The Virginia delegates wish to withdraw for discussion," one stated, and they went aside. Ultimately 10 states favored organization. Mississippi and Virginia abstained, although it was painful to do so. There were troubles with their state conventions, and it would be worse if they dared to affiliate with the new Executive Committee of Woman's Mission Societies, Auxiliary to the Southern Baptist Convention.

Mrs. Whitfield apparently could no longer take the strain on her nerves. She asked to be excused from presiding and looked almost comically relieved when Annie took her place. Annie led the women to vote on the constitution, one article at a time. There were two sessions on Monday, and changes were made to the constitution in both sessions. At the end of the day, however, they had a working constitution, a stated purpose, and a slate of officers. Martha McIntosh was elected president. Annie was elected corresponding secretary. These two women, with their very different strengths, would complement the other.

With Martha as chair, a nominating committee selected the other officers: Mrs. Pollard was recording secretary and Mrs. John Pullen was treasurer. Along with these officers there were vice-presidents, one from each state, and a board of local managers.

"While the Maryland Mission Rooms are separate from the Executive Committee of the Woman's Mission Societies, the committee is welcome to the use of the rooms for meetings, as well as access to the reading room literature,"

Annie offered. The women accepted. This meant the local board of managers would all be Baltimore women: Alice Armstrong, Mrs. F. M. Ellis, Mrs. James Tyler, Mrs. J. H. Brittain, Mrs. O. F. Gregory, Mrs. J. J. G. Riley, Miss Addie Wilson, Mrs. W. J. Brown, and Miss Lily Graves. This board of managers was crucial, for they would conduct the business of the organization between annual meetings. It would not be possible for all the vice-presidents to travel to Baltimore every time there was business to conduct. The vice-presidents were really more of an advisory board.

The women made sure everyone present understood the Executive Committee's purposes: It existed to distribute missionary information and stimulate missions effort, and it existed to collect and raise funds for missions. The women, as they always had, emphasized they wanted to work with the Southern Baptist Convention and the mission boards. They were not in the business of appointing their own missionaries or disbursing funds. Since they wished to work beside the boards, they would ask the boards to pay their expenses. They would keep nothing for themselves, turning all money raised over to the boards. What they required in reimbursements should be a small percentage compared to what they could raise. Annie and Martha were appointed to confer with the boards on behalf of the Executive Committee.

While Annie was opinionated, she also cared about the opinions of others. As she stood before the women she asked, "What are your marching orders?"

The first marching order was to undertake a request by Mr. Tichenor of the Home Mission Board. He was not about to lose an opportunity to enlist the women's help, and had already written a letter to be read at the meeting. Would the women raise funds for a church building and cemetery lot in Cuba? They certainly would.

Exhilarated by what had occurred, Annie couldn't wait to get home and tell the rest of her family all about it. She knew they had been praying for her and for the meeting. But first she spent a blissful day hearing reports from the missionaries. Mina Everett of Brazil spoke, as did Mrs. Sallie Holmes, a veteran co-worker of Martha Crawford and Lottie Moon. Annie was especially pleased to see Lula Whilden, home on furlough. So much had happened since that prayer service for her and the other missionaries at Eutaw Place.

Finally Alice and Annie boarded the train for Baltimore, tired, happy, and ready to go forward. They quickly found, however, that there were still critics who feared them. The June 7 issue of the Kentucky state paper, the *Western Recorder*, tried to make the case that the organization was a splinter group of unsatisfied women.

"We, the women of the churches" should have been written, "We, the handful of the women," the paper said.

They had tried reassuring the brethren with articles, with statements by men with the stature of Ellis, Tichenor, and Tupper, with the clause in the preamble that said, "disclaiming all intention of independent action." None of it had been enough. As the new leader, she felt that if the women started work at once and showed their cooperation with the boards, much criticism would be silenced. With that in mind, she threw herself heart and soul into a work that would become for 18 years her whole life.

5

The Early Years of WMU

Annie had no intention of losing the momentum built up in their May meeting. She was eager to start on the Cuba project, as were the other delegates. The groundwork had been laid a year earlier, when the Maryland Woman's Home Mission Society had made Cuba a new department of work. The Maryland Missions Committee had also already decided if the women did not organize in Richmond, they would distribute the brick cards printed by the Home Mission Board.

The brick cards were a novel idea. The women enjoyed reading the front panel, which contained facts about Cuba and the need for a church building. There was even a picture of Alberto Diaz, pastor of First Baptist Church, Havana. The two inside panels were covered with 20 pictures of little bricks. Each time someone donated 10 cents, his or her name went on one of the bricks. When the bricks were full, it meant $2.00 had been collected.

Annie, though she could stick with tedious, mind-numbing details, always enjoyed a new approach to doing missions work. After the Richmond meeting, she was passionate about seeing the project through to completion.

Her job was to make sure the brick cards were mailed to the state committees, so they could in turn give them to church societies.

"Miss Annie must like these brick cards," one volunteer said to the other after they had begun the project.

"What makes you say that?" the other volunteer asked.

"I can't imagine her mailing out 11,000 of the things if she didn't like them," came the weary response.

Miss Annie did love the mail, it was agreed. One day, a veteran volunteer overheard Miss Annie training a novice. She was showing the woman how to attach stamps so they would look "just-so" rather than slapdash. "Now, dearie," she said kindly as she lectured on the importance of neatness, "remember, first impressions are always the most important."

The veteran leaned over and whispered to a co-worker, "Wait till she gives her the lecture on saving string." As much as Annie loved the mail, she did not love spending the boards' expense money, which she considered a sacred trust. She sent her many parcels by freight whenever possible and preached the virtues of thrift in office management.

Annie kept the mails busy with her letters not only to Tupper and Tichenor, but also to the state committees. She sent them advice and information about what other states were doing. She also sent a copy of each piece of literature to the state central committees, which would then order what they wanted and send it along to the societies in that state. As the months went by, the orders rolled in more frequently.

"Look, Alice!" she cried one day after totaling up orders, "I have sent Mississippi 30 pounds of literature in the past six months!" For a state so recently organized, this was a sterling achievement and showed Annie that the Mississippi women were serious about missions.

October 1888

Not wanting to shortchange foreign missions, Annie had approached Dr. Tupper in July about a foreign missions project that would interest the women. In her heart of hearts, Annie did not like working with the Foreign Mission Board secretary. When she could, she directed her comments and questions to the assistant secretary and editor of the *Foreign Mission Journal*, Dr. T. P. Bell. He was closer to Annie's age, and she enjoyed trading ideas with him.

When asked why she didn't like working with Dr. Tupper, Annie would only say, "He does not understand the women's work. He throws obstacles in the way, though perhaps not with intent to hinder. I find it exceedingly difficult to consult with him on important matters." Still, he was the head of the Board, and Annie worked with him. He was ready for her newest request, and sent her a letter from Lottie Moon dated May 24 which petitioned for women workers for the field of P'ingtu. It was really not so much a petition as a cry for help.

Lottie Moon, who unlike her sister, Eddie, had proven a champion on the missions field, was on the verge of exhaustion. She refused, however, to leave China for a furlough until other trained missionaries arrived to continue her work. Dr. Tupper told Annie, "The only hope of China is through the women."

This was just the thing, Annie felt. She presented the letter to the women at the October executive meeting. Tupper had informed her that it would cost $2,000 to send two women missionaries. There was no point in trying to send only one. Eddie Moon, who had sailed for China as an energetic, idealistic young woman, had returned home a mental and physical wreck. Single women missionaries needed a partner.

The women agreed to raise the money to send two missionaries. This was what they had been hoping for—to help in greater ways. But how would they go about raising the money? This would take more than the beloved mite box offering to accomplish.

"I have a suggestion," Annie began, to no one's great surprise. "Miss Moon has already suggested we have a week of self-denial at the Christmas season. Why not time the offering for then?" The women were pleased. Christians were more likely to pray and think of Jesus during the time of His birth, so it was a perfect fit. The offering would be brought in on January 9, during the World Week of Prayer.

The Executive Committee instructed Annie to begin the fund-raising by preparing and distributing the literature the women always needed. Annie called in her faithful volunteers and sent out 3,000 circular letters from Martha McIntosh to the societies; 3,000 programs for the January 9 meeting; 30,000 offering envelopes, for both the women and the Sunday Schools; and 1,000 notices about how to order envelopes. This effort cost the Foreign Mission Board exactly $72.82.

As Annie began the New Year 1889 and looked back on 1888, she was pleased with the way the work had gone. Not only had the women organized in Richmond, but also Mississippi had joined the Union in the same year. Offerings were good and requests for literature were pouring in. Annie had written 637 letters and 182 postcards.

"If only Jane were alive to know of all this" was Annie's one sad thought as she said good-bye to the old year. Jane Norris Graves, the girlhood friend who had gone to China as the bride of Rosewell Graves in 1872, had died in 1888.

Annie rallied her spirits quickly. It was wrong to become despondent when God had blessed so much. It was a new year and new work lay ahead. "Go forward!" she told herself. There was the ingathering of the offering on January 9 to think of.

The World Week of Prayer came and went. To her delight, Annie was able to report that the women brought in $3,315.26, enough money for three missionaries.

North China, Winter 1889

In a pleasant, neatly kept room a tiny woman sat at a desk reading a letter from her dear Dr. Tupper at the Foreign Mission Board. Her clothes were a mixture of Chinese and Western styles, and her dark hair was pulled back tightly. She had the stature of a child but the worn face of someone exhausted in mind and body. After she read the news that Southern Baptist women had raised enough money to send three missionaries to help her, she laid her head on the desk and said a prayer of thanksgiving.

"I can hold on now," whispered Lottie Moon to herself. "I can hold on now that I know help is on the way."

Annual Meeting, Memphis, 1889

Pastor Diaz from Cuba had come all the way to Memphis to thank the women for their support of the work in Cuba. Dr. Tichenor had sent a letter of thanks to be read aloud. The women were happy to continue supporting the Cuba work.

Martha McIntosh, having been prodded by Annie, gave her first presidential address. "You have selected one of your own number to preside at this meeting—one of like weakness with yourselves—but let us remember that the King Himself is with us, the meek and lowly Jesus." The women immediately warmed to the modest, deeply spiritual nature of their president. She reviewed the work they had done that year; but among the successes, she admitted areas of neglect, especially work with children.

"We could only make the beginning in this line of work," she told the women, owing to all the rush of getting organized. Alice had produced a leaflet, titled "Our Duty to Young People," to help in the children's work. The women were happy to have it, and to have the manual of how to organize and operate, which had been published prior to the meeting. It was called "Chips from Many Workshops" and was chock-full of ideas.

Annie rose to address the women. She was not like the contemplative Martha. She had more the aura of a general rallying her troops. They had done well, they knew. Besides all the projects supported and funds raised, WMU material was now appearing in the *Foreign Mission Journal* courtesy of Alice Armstrong, and the organization was sending data to the *Heathen Helper* and the *Baptist Basket*. But they needed to do more. Annie reminded them that offerings still came to about 5 cents each annually for missions.

"We must unite," she told them. Painting a word picture of leaders holding high the banners for their followers, she told them the one word that could be their motto: Forward! How could the women not respond? Annie, their leader, worked sweatshop hours and refused any salary whatsoever. With her as their example, they could only forge ahead.

Baltimore, January 1890

A bearded man in his 60s, distinguished and obviously a gentleman, greeted the Executive Committee members as they entered the mission rooms. Dr. Tichenor had traveled from Atlanta to Baltimore to confer with WMU leaders and discuss suggestions for work. At this meeting, Dr. Tichenor wished to discuss frontier boxes.

As was her habit, Miss Annie had written and asked him about the subject; but now it was his job to encourage or discourage the women. He had no intention of discouraging them. The boxes of clothing and other goods they wished to send to frontier missionaries could make all the difference in the lives of these families, many of whom were destitute. The value of one missionary box or barrel could equal one-fourth a frontier missionary's yearly salary!

The one thing Dr. Tichenor would not do was tell the societies which missionaries should receive boxes. To do so would open the Home Mission Board to all kinds of charges of favoritism. The Board would, however, endorse the work, and he would appeal directly to the women at the Annual Meeting coming up in Fort Worth in the spring.

Fort Worth, May 1890

Dr. Tichenor, as Annie knew he would, kept his word and wrote a letter that kindled a passion for frontier boxes.

"It is a fact that many of our missionaries labor on the frontier and elsewhere, are very inadequately paid for their services, undergoing many privations. They are exposed to all of the changes of weather, winter and summer, in our changeful climate. To meet their appointments, they ofttimes face cold, storm and darkness, swim swollen rivers, sleep in houses through which whistle the wintry blasts, preach in winter without fires and in summer without shelters; and are thus dying daily for the Master and souls of men. The families of these hearty pioneers undergo equal privations. In the long absence of husband and father, they are often left without protection and without adequate supplies of food or clothing. Their children are growing up without social advantages, and without books or opportunities for mental improvement. These men are laying the foundations of our denominational prosperity, are the burden bearers, the real heros of our missionary force. In these frontier fields are to be found the real hardships of missionary life, at home or abroad."

How could the women not approve a recommendation to send frontier boxes after hearing that epistle? After the meeting, as the train rolled out of Texas, a woman with a deep southern accent approached Annie. She introduced herself as Annie Grace Tartt of Livingston, Alabama. The two Annies fell to talking about frontier boxes.

"Could you possibly supply me with the name of a frontier missionary right away?" her new friend asked. She couldn't wait to get started on the project. In this way

Alabama, which had organized for missions in 1889, got in on the ground floor of frontier box work. Annie was delighted.

Summer 1890

The frontier box project continued to thrive. She had the frontier missionaries' names, and the society would find out specifically what its missionary needed. At one point she had more requests than she had names, and Dr. Tichenor supplied more, without, of course, indicating which he thought were more deserving. Of course, it wasn't perfect. Some societies took names of missionaries, and Annie would learn later, to her grief and irritation, that no boxes were ever sent. Also, some women seemed to think that frontier missionaries were so desperate that they would be glad to have junk and castoffs that the church women in the East no longer wanted and that served no earthly good. The fact that there were problems was no excuse for stopping a work that helped so many missionaries, Annie reminded herself. And, the boxes gave women such a personal connection to the frontier missionaries.

One of Annie's goals was to strengthen the connection between the frontier and the older parts of the Southern Baptist Convention. She worked hard to begin mission societies among frontier women. They, too, had a responsibility to support all the missions endeavors, not just their own.

As Annie worked in a happy whirl of literature orders, letters, and state reports, she was one day stopped short by a letter from the Missouri Central Committee. Along with the report on Missouri's collection for a chapel in Rio de Janeiro, the women asked the national WMU's help. They wanted them to observe a special day when collections would be taken for the building fund.

The national organization had led in a special offering before, for women missionaries, but the offering was at the Foreign Mission Board's request. While offerings for mission chapels was a popular project for both home and foreign fields, Annie wasn't sure about the propriety of the women advocating a project. It hinted at the women dictating to the boards, the very appearance Annie and the other leaders wanted to avoid.

Still, Missouri was a divided state. Northern Baptists had work in the state as well. What if the women left the work completely? That would be a terrible loss.

"This is a perfect opportunity to interest the women in the general work," she said to herself as she mulled over the situation. "I shall write to Dr. Tupper," she finally decided.

Dr. Tupper's reply did nothing to help her anxiety. His letter read, "The best thing, in the matter of foreign missions, the men and women of the country can do in my judgment is to raise money for the Board and let the Board appropriate it."

Annie turned to Martha for help. They agreed to ask Dr. Tupper to reconsider, since they both feared losing Missouri. His next letter seemed hurriedly written, almost like a telegram. Apparently he was going on a trip and had dashed off the letter. "Unable to communicate with the Board in time, the corresponding secretary will assume the responsibility of endorsing the judgment of the Executive Committee about acceding to the request of the Missouri ladies, provided you do not prefer to wait more formal action on my return."

"Well, there's the go-ahead," Annie thought. She wrote another letter for more specific instructions, but received no reply. Considering that Dr. Tupper had said he would "assume the responsibility," WMU moved ahead; and with the Missouri Central Committee set a date for next March for the offering.

Richmond, November 1890

"The Board has never approved the chapel, Miss Armstrong." For once, Annie was speechless as she took in what Dr. Tupper was saying. She had come to Richmond to ask, among other things, for more specific instructions about the planned offering for the Rio chapel. After all the letters, now he was saying the Board hadn't even decided to build it yet!

When she began to express her surprise, Dr. Tupper said, "Miss Armstrong, the Board does not tell its plans until it is decided what is to be done." Annie's thoughts buzzed. WMU had publicly asked for money for something the Board had not definitely decided upon . . . the embarrassment of looking as if they did not know what they were doing . . . the field day the critics would have who charged that WMU tried to influence the boards. Somehow, Annie managed to end the interview, but she did not end the subject of the Rio chapel.

After returning home, she wrote to Foreign Mission Board president H. H. Harris: "Pardon me if I seem to be calling in question Dr. Tupper's judgment in this matter, but I do believe very thoroughly if our work is to amount to anything, we must not be placed in a position where it would be very clearly seen that we do not know what we are about."

December 1890

Upon learning that Dr. Tupper had secured Board approval for the Rio chapel, Annie wrote him to ask how much money WMU could spend on literature for the offering. She then wrote to T. P. Bell for other advice. Everything had turned out all right, but it could have been a fiasco; and Annie filed the experience away in her keen and ample memory.

Still, as she reflected on the year, it had been a good one. She was 40 years old and just moving into her prime as corresponding secretary. She had written 2,737 letters on behalf of missions that year. True, the effort had damaged her hand, but perhaps it was only temporary. Now that the boards had authorized the purchase of a typewriter and a clerk, she would not have to strain her hand so much. She could put more effort into the rest of the work.

She ticked off the year's accomplishments. North Carolina had joined WMU. There was home missions work in west Arkansas. WMU was helping a girls' school in Cuba. More women's societies were forming all the time.

WMU was finding wider avenues of reaching children. Dr. Samuel Boykin, the editor of the Home Mission Board Sunday School paper, *Kind Words,* had offered WMU space in the series. The committee had first discussed the possibility of a column with Dr. Tichenor at their October meeting. The Executive Committee hesitated to accept this offer, fearing to spread too thin, but finally accepted. Annie was glad they had. After all, what a wonderful way of getting missions information to children.

The missionary boxes were another bright spot. Societies had sent almost $4,500 worth of goods in 71 boxes to missionaries as close by as North Carolina and as far away as Idaho.

Annie greeted the year 1891 wondering what other good work God had in store for WMU to do.

1891

"Miss Annie, why don't you sit for your picture? The women would love to know what their leader looks like." The lady who made this kind suggestion was only repeating a request made many times over. Annie gave her usual reply.

"Thank you, but I do not have my picture taken. What if some man found a copy of it and took it into a saloon? A woman should be spared the humiliation of such public stares, even in print."

If anyone thought the chance of Annie's picture ending up a saloon to be unlikely, they did not voice that opinion to her. She, likewise, did not tell more than a few trusted people the real reason for her refusal to have a picture made.

One year, at the Home of the Friendless, Annie put on a huge Christmas party for the orphans. She organized a Christmas celebration every year, but this particular year she had had 1,000 invitations sent out to the children of Baltimore, asking them to bring something for the orphans. As a special treat, she arranged for a stereopticon presentation. As she worked she happily imagined the wonder the children would feel at seeing a real "magic lantern" show.

She had taken a break from her work to have a portrait made; and when things calmed down, she planned to pick up her picture from the photographer. The portrait had been made for a certain missionary gentleman. . . . Annie quickly broke off those thoughts to concentrate on the present.

Her friend who had teased her on the sidewalk that summer day had made good on his promise to come help her. He was assisting this very Christmas with the stereopticon (projector for transparent slides) show. As the children oohed and aahed over the images projected onto the curtain, Annie felt her own heart swell with pleasure. She had always loved making children happy.

Suddenly the room erupted in squeals and giggles. Cries of "Miss Annie! Miss Annie!" arose. She looked, and to her horror and disbelief, there was a portrait on the screen. Was it of herself? Yes, it was she! For her picture she had worn a high-collared dress with a lace ruffle around it, and a locket on a gold chain. Her abundant dark brown hair had been put up and ornamented with a comb.

How could such a disaster happen? She discovered her friend had gotten her picture from the photographer and made a slide to slip in during the show. He had meant it only as a lark. She shook her head to clear away the embarrassing memory. There were other details of the event that, though everyone else found humorous, she still found mortifying. On that day she had sworn *never* to have her picture made again.

Birmingham, May 1891

At the Annual Meeting T. T. Eaton, editor of the *Western Recorder*, was present in his capacity as chairman of the Centennial Committee. His task was to invite WMU, SBC, to stir up the churches to more liberal giving to missions as a way of marking the 100th anniversary of the modern missionary movement. In the year 1792, a British shoemaker named William Carey had gone to India as a missionary, and his life and work had helped kindle the modern missionary movement. To honor the centennial, the Southern Baptist Convention wanted to increase the foreign missions force by 100 and improve all its missionary work.

The Kentucky newspaper editor asked WMU to focus its efforts on reaching children and youth, launching a missions education campaign, and distributing leaflets and tracts. And, would the women also raise $250,000 to build chapels and mission houses? While the women were agreeable to everything, Annie and the Executive Committee did not wish to promise $250,000. Instead, they hedged their answer by saying they would raise as much of it as possible.

Other big things were happening at the larger Southern Baptist Convention. The Convention had just voted to establish its own Sunday School Board, to be located in Nashville, Tennessee. Annie rejoiced at the news. For once she was in a different corner from her beloved family and church, who supported the American Baptist Publication Society. Annie wanted Southern Baptists to have their own Sunday School literature, and to be dependent on the Northern Baptists for nothing.

James Marion Frost was appointed corresponding secretary of the Sunday School Board, and Annie added him to her growing list of correspondents. Soon she was writing material for the quarterly curriculum. Sometimes her name was on the material as writer, sometimes not.

Recognition for herself did not matter. Southern Baptists having their own Sunday School materials did.

While she was glad about the Sunday School Board, she was sorry to learn that Martha McIntosh would not accept another term as WMU president. The name Fannie Heck was often dropped in discussions of who would succeed Martha. Fannie was now president of the North Carolina Woman's Missionary Union, which had only organized in 1890. Martha herself had picked Fannie as her successor. Annie also approved.

With her usual forthrightness, Annie wrote her to ask if she would she accept the presidency if the ladies desired it. She would.

Then WMU, SBC, sent a letter to China missionary Lottie Moon, who had finally arrived in Virginia on furlough. Would she come to see them? She would not.

Miss Moon's refusal was disappointing, but she could hardly be faulted for it. She had held on heroically until new missionaries could arrive in North China. The missionaries already there were dying around her at a horrific rate. She was at one point single-handedly holding together Southern Baptist missions in North China, while beset on every side by people begging for her preaching and teaching. She needed several months of rest before she could begin traveling and speaking.

Annie settled down to work the rest of 1891 and into 1892 with the projects WMU had already begun—the centennial effort, missionary boxes, some publications work, teaching stewardship and organization, supporting the work in Cuba, and raising money to support women missionaries in China. So much had been accomplished; but she felt as she prayed and listened for God's leading, that there was much, much more to be done.

6
Personal Interests

Baltimore, One Sunday Morning, 1892

"Annie, are you staying home from church?" Her mother looked unhappily at the pile of paperwork in front of Annie. It was Sunday morning and Annie was not dressed in hat, gloves, and high-top shoes as she should have been.

"There are so many letters to get out, Mother. I simply must keep pegging away," Annie replied, half-apologetically.

Her mother left her alone. Not only did she dislike Annie missing church, but she feared her youngest daughter was overworking. Usually the only day out of the year when Annie gave herself a break from work was Christmas Day. Annie, however, was a grown woman, too old for Mary to tell her what to do. Besides, she told herself, it was a very rare occasion when Annie skipped church.

After the house was quiet, Annie went back to her writing. At the mission rooms, she could use a typewriter or have a clerk type letters for her; but on weekends or while traveling, she still wrote by hand. She wrote to Dr. Tupper, Dr. Tichenor, and Dr. Frost at least twice a week, sometimes more. She wanted them to know everything that was going on with WMU, and she wanted to know about their work. Poor men, they worked so hard, she told herself. How their families must miss them. That reminded her of something, and she picked up her pen to add a line to a letter.

"How is your dear family?" she wrote. She wanted "the brethren," as she called them, to know that "Miss Annie" cared about them as people, not just administrators.

After awhile, she had to stop and rest her hand, which was still somewhat weakened from all the writing she had done in the days before typewriters. Since this year, 1892, was the Centennial of Missions, there had been an extra amount of correspondence. She had put a lot of thought into the best way to raise money for the centennial. There had been a special week of prayer in January. WMU, SBC, had made certificates of stock in the Centennial Chapel Building Fund at $5.00 a share. The paper looked like a real stock certificate, but bore the picture of William Carey, the dates 1792 and 1892, and the words *Centennial Chapel Building Fund.* The good old brick cards also came back into use.

The mission boards had made an appeal in the state papers in February. Right after that appeal was printed, WMU sent the materials to women's societies. All materials going to Sunday Schools for the Children's Day programs were mailed out by the Maryland Mission Rooms. While these mailing were going on, stories were printed in the Baptist papers about the need for chapels and mission houses. The stories had been written by the missionaries themselves. Annie had worked long hours, and would work more, compiling mailing lists; preparing literature; editing articles; and, as always, writing letters.

Even though Annie was in charge of WMU and the mission rooms, she wanted it understood that the Maryland Mission Rooms had sent the material to Sunday Schools. Unfortunately, it made no difference to the critics. Annie and the other women suffered the accusations that they were leaving the sphere of women by sending out material for the whole church, not just the women.

Also, WMU was criticized for making the chapel appeal before the mission boards had made their general appeal. This was also unjust because Annie had consulted closely with the boards on the timing of the appeal.

"Well, we must go forward, criticism or no," she told herself as she started another letter. Just then Mary and Alice returned home from church and filled Annie in on the details of the service. Dr. Ellis had asked after her, but had not seemed upset when told she was working at home.

Annie excused herself from the lunch table and went back to work. There were so many matters with which to deal—printers, manuscripts, questions from state committees, letters to missionaries. She must take care of those matters today, for the next week was full of speaking engagements and an all-day quarterly meeting for the Maryland Home Mission Society. Also, Mamie and her family were traveling, which meant Annie must fill in for Mamie as treasurer of the Maryland Foreign Mission Society. There were orders to fill for the Maryland Mission Rooms as well as for WMU, SBC.

As she made lists of everything she had to do, and which organization the work was for, she was reminded of an odd question a woman had asked her.

"Miss Annie," the woman had said wonderingly, "Do you never get confused about all the different roles you fill?" What a funny thing that was to ask. There was no need to get confused if one simply worked in a regular, orderly fashion until all the tasks were done. It seemed so patently obvious to Annie.

Atlanta, May 1892

Fannie Heck stood at the podium of the WMU Annual Meeting, receiving the adoration of the women in the audience. She was not quite 30 years old and had an aura of modest southern beauty about her. Only a few of the women in the meeting knew that Fannie Heck was, as the old saying went, "an iron hand in a velvet glove."

To Fannie's delight, one of her first tasks as president was to introduce Lottie Moon to the women. Miss Moon had rested several months at her sister's home, and then come out full force in her efforts to rouse Southern Baptists' interest in missions.

"Here is our heroic missionary," Fannie said to the women, who thrilled to the sight of a tiny woman in Chinese robes standing before them. While she spoke of her 19 years in China, of the changing attitudes of the people, of the intellect of the Chinese, and of the hunger for the gospel, Annie and her new president became listeners among a throng of other listeners. For that time, Annie faded into the background.

September 1892

"Well, we can't always be on the mountaintop with the likes of Miss Moon," Annie told herself in the midst of packing boxes. WMU's national office was moving to 9 West Lexington Street, and there was a quantity of detailed organization to do in moving all the literature and other material.

March 1893

It was the centennial celebration of Baptists in Richmond. Annie was attending with Mrs. Pollard as her traveling companion. Annie would again hear Lottie Moon speak on foreign missions while she, Annie, would speak on why home missions should be a part of the centennial movement.

"There are three reasons why home missions should be included in the centennial," Annie began, when it was her time to speak to the women. "God is bringing the nations of the world to America. By helping home missions, the foreign supply is increased. The need for chapels and other aid, especially on the frontier, is immediate and distressing." Annie elaborated on those three points, grateful especially for the opportunity to speak again about frontier needs.

Later there was a missionary tea and the two women, so different in physical appearance but so alike in dedication and energy, shared another experience. They had their hands almost wrung off by crowds who wished to shake their hands and say they had met them.

Nashville, May 1893

Annie could scarcely believe it was time for the Annual Meeting again. Miss Moon would again be joining them. That, at least, would be a bright spot. The report on the centennial chapel offering would hardly compare. After all her work and the work of the state central committees and mission boards, WMU's contributions from May 1892 to last month were $62,326.75. Eutaw Place by itself had set an offering of $15,000, which it had met. "Because Eugene and Joshua gave two-thirds that amount," Annie thought more than once.

At the meeting, the women craned their necks for a glimpse of Miss Moon, but soon found that she was happy to take her place among them in worship and business discussion. She was in favor of WMU cooperating with the Sunday School Board in sponsoring Missionary Day for Sunday School. Not surprisingly, she wanted WMU to seek to raise funds to support all women missionaries. When the topic of the Christmas offering came up, however, she did surprise many of the 57 delegates by endorsing the use of the offering to support work in Japan rather than her beloved China.

It was her loving discourse on China, however, that moved the women's hearts. She spoke of faithful Chinese, martyred for Christ. She told of the rich rewards of missions work. She tried to give to the WMU delegates the experience of all her time in China, all in one message to them. The women could not just sit passively. Fannie Breedlove Davis of Texas put her arm around the veteran missionary and said with tenderness, "You have been the inspiration of my life." Then she looked at the delegates and in a stronger voice declared, "She has given her life! What must she think of us? Shall we come up next year with such a small sum?"

Not only did Lottie Moon's words inspire the women, they did a great deal to refute the claims being made even by some WMU supporters about the Gospel Mission movement. As Annie moved among the women at the meeting, she picked up bits and pieces of discussion about it. She was alert to this issue because if it carried the day, it would mean the dismantling of the mission boards. She would do everything in her power to keep that from happening.

Lottie Moon was also aware of the Gospel Mission movement. She could not help but be aware of it, since veteran China missionary T. P. Crawford was fanning the flames of this new movement. Other women heard one side's views, then the other's. There was much confusion.

"I don't understand this Gospel Mission movement," one delegate said to another during the dinner hour.

"From what I can tell, it advocates self-support for missionaries," her partner answered. "They say that the boards are an unnecessary administrative expense, and are unbiblical since the Bible doesn't say anything about mission boards."

"Oh, well, that's true," the delegate said hesitantly.

"It doesn't say anything about WMU, SBC, in the Bible either. Does that mean we shouldn't exist?" the other woman said indignantly.

The whole Gospel Mission movement gave many people headaches. Finally, Dr. Tupper, who had borne the brunt of fighting the Gospel Mission's criticism of the Foreign Mission Board while at the same time trying to keep Lottie

Moon from breaking down or resigning before her furlough, had had enough. He was in his 70s. It was time to retire. Many people, including Lottie Moon, were sorry to see him go. Annie was not.

"I feel the greatest relief in Dr. Tupper's resignation," she told close friends. She had never felt she could get enough direction from Dr. Tupper, and the thought of the Rio chapel still rankled.

Annie had tried for a long while to avoid dealing with Dr. Tupper, and was grateful for Dr. T. P. Bell, who was prompt in answering her letters. When the secretaries procrastinated in answering her, Annie was prone to nag and even send telegrams, though she would apologize for it later. There was no need for that with Dr. Bell. "If it had not been for the help Dr. T. P. Bell gave, I think it would have been utterly impossible for us to have persevered in our work," she told those who cared to listen. She had wanted Dr. Bell to become Dr. Tupper's successor, but instead found he was going to be the corresponding secretary of the Sunday School Board.

"Who is going to succeed Dr. Tupper?" she asked, and was told it was R. J. Willingham, who had pastored in Tennessee and Georgia. Annie barely knew him, and wrote him at once about the relationship between WMU and the Board.

"Please visit Baltimore as soon as possible," she urged in the letter. She even offered to go to Richmond, as much as she detested the travel. It would be worth it to have a personal conference.

Meanwhile, she needed to prepare for Missionary Day in Sunday School, set for October 15. The mission boards had asked that WMU inaugurate such a day, when children would receive missionary training and there would be a collection for missions, to be divided evenly between home and foreign missions.

"I want this to be done well," Annie said to her co-workers and the Board secretaries. Annie wanted the Board secretaries to make the appeal to the churches, so WMU could not be criticized for bossing the churches. She, however, prepared the circular, the letter introducing the day, the program itself, and a pyramid-shaped mite box. The box would be given out on Missionary Day, and the offering brought in on Thanksgiving, or the Sunday before or after. Annie was gratified by the amount of literature the churches ordered. She felt the first annual Missionary Day in Sunday School would go well.

Baltimore, October 1893

When Annie walked into the Maryland Baptist Union Association meeting, she was delighted to see the new Foreign Mission Board secretary there as well. In between meetings, she squeezed in as much time as possible with him. Unfortunately, other people kept wanting his time, so their talk was brief and interrupted, and Annie was not at all satisfied.

Baltimore, Winter 1894

"Yes, by all means write Secretary Willingham on our behalf and invite him." This was all Annie was waiting for—the instructions from the WMU Executive Committee to invite Willingham to come to Baltimore and the Board's recommendations for the upcoming WMU Annual Meeting. She wrote him and waited for a reply. And waited. And waited.

"Has any letter from Richmond come?" became a regular question at mail time, and the answer was always no. Or, if a letter did come, the secretary was putting off the committee, saying he was too busy or was hindered. It did not occur to Annie that as the new secretary learning his position at the Board, and facing the Gospel Mission threat as well as mounting debt, that he had many other things on his mind.

One day Willingham received another letter from Annie, quite blunt in tone, in which she accused him of having a low estimate of the work done by those in charge of both WMU and the Maryland Mission Rooms. She told him how disappointed she was at not making more progress in the work.

"You did not come to Baltimore at the time spoken of; and when you were in Baltimore in October, it was the most hurried kind of talk we had together, and I must say to the Secretary of the WMU altogether unsatisfactory." She added, speaking of him in the third person, "I have never felt that Dr. Willingham understood the Woman's Work."

In consternation, Willingham read her next question: Was it too much for them to expect him to come and familiarize himself with the work they were doing?

"What does this woman want from me?" he thought. In his opinion, he had spent more time writing to her and attending to her letters than he had any other individual. And, he would write and tell her so!

He quickly received a reply. No, he hadn't given her an adequate amount of time, she wrote. She had compared her correspondence to him with his correspondence to her. She had sent more letters, cards, and telegrams. Willingham waved the white flag of surrender, and packed his bag for Baltimore. He met with Annie and the Executive Committee in February.

For awhile, Annie tried not to write to him too often after that. She didn't want him to say she was monopolizing his time. Besides, she had many other things to concentrate on, such as Fannie Heck.

Fannie Heck had done some work as WMU president, but her own health and the health of her family kept her from making the trip to Baltimore very often. She had come to a couple of Executive Committee meetings and other events, and had presided at the 1893 Annual Meeting. She also supplied the material for the Sunbeam

Department in the *Foreign Mission Journal.* She wanted to be kept informed on the work, and gave advice and her opinion through letters.

Annie thought a great deal of Fannie Heck. She was gifted and wanted to serve God. She had heard that the president was being sent to Philadelphia in March for medical treatment, and planned to go see her to persuade her to continue in the office.

Meanwhile, Annie needed Dr. Bell to send her the recommendations from the Sunday School Board now that she finally had Dr. Willingham's. She wrote to him, asking him to send them along in time for the Annual Meeting in May.

After Annie finished writing Dr. Bell, she flipped open one of her notebooks and went over notes she had made. The Home Mission Board had appointed Marie Buhlmaier to work with the German immigrants arriving in Baltimore. She had arrived last October and Annie had quickly become friends with her. Annie needed to request from the Sunday School Board more Bibles, Testaments, and tracts for Marie. A steady stream of immigrants flowed into Baltimore because of its great port. The needs of the immigrants tugged at Annie's heart. She was always interested in their welfare and Marie's work with them.

She continued scanning her notes. Many blacks lived in Baltimore. Besides supporting the work of already-established black churches, Annie wanted to start new work. Black and white leaders together wanted to start an orphanage for black children. Baptist women were starting sewing circles and the same kind of mothers' meetings that Annie had begun for poor women in her neighborhood. Those meetings were in the educational rooms at Eutaw Place. Annie scribbled a reminder to herself to ask the Sunday School Board to send literature to home missionaries working with the black population.

The next item on her list was young people's work. Last year at the Southern Baptist Convention there had been discussion of starting a young people's union. This in part was in self-defense, for the Northern Baptist Young People's Union of America (more briefly known as BYPUA), which had formed in 1891, had already formed a Southern Department. It was a very popular organization, and Annie feared southern young people would be attracted to it. She felt it put talking over working, which went against everything she had been taught.

On the other hand, an organization that helped young Southern Baptists connect to the Convention would be a good thing—provided missions was prominent in it. She made a note to herself to write some letters on this subject.

Annie closed her notebook with a sigh. There were so many good and interesting works to do—immigrants, frontier work, Indians, orphans, mountain schools, mothers' meetings. And she had to put it all aside and tackle something very unpleasant: the Gospel Mission movement. It had appeared in full strength in Georgia WMU. She must help the state WMUs. It was part of her job as corresponding secretary. She would go to Richmond often, and to the District of Columbia, and was willing to go anywhere else she was needed, although travel was odious to her. Not as odious, however, as losing support for the mission boards or losing territory for Southern Baptists. She started planning her strategy.

7
Altercations with Annie

When Annie met with Fannie Heck to talk about the upcoming Annual Meeting, she was struck by how unwell the president looked. While Annie knew the younger woman had been ill, she did not realize the emotional trauma that was at the root of much of Fannie Heck's sickness. Her darling father had passed away, and she had broken down from the grief and stress. That trauma, combined with already existing physical illness, had caused Fannie Heck's frailty. All Annie realized was that Fannie Heck was in Philadelphia for medical treatment, and they had WMU business that must be discussed.

Like Annie, the president was dedicated and selfless. Fannie Heck ignored her own illness long enough to meet with Annie. But when the women discussed the recommendations from the boards, it became obvious the two women were not alike in their opinions of WMU work with the boards.

"Why are we even entertaining recommendations from the Sunday School Board?" Fannie demanded. "Who asked Dr. Bell for recommendations?"

Annie dodged the question about Dr. Bell. "As an auxiliary to the Convention, WMU should support the work of all the boards," she argued.

"I disagree," Fannie responded. "The Sunday School Board is opposed by some; they will not approve of WMU helping the Board. And if we help the Sunday School Board, should we not expect Southern Seminary to ask for assistance next?"

"They already have," Annie thought, though she certainly was not going to share that information with Fannie. Southern Seminary had made overtures to Annie for WMU's help, but Annie had made no promises to them.

"I think opposition to the Sunday School Board is fading," she said. "Besides, Southern Seminary is not a board, therefore it has not the same claim upon us that the Convention's boards have."

Fannie pressed that other people might not see it that way. Annie did not argue. Fannie was obviously in no shape to attend the Annual Meeting, and was not going to be reelected, so the matter would die of itself. Or so she thought.

Dallas, May 1894

"I have called this meeting to discuss the Gospel Mission movement." Annie got the attention of state central committee members instantly with those words. The movement was affecting women's work in Georgia, Kentucky, and the Carolinas. The committee members in other states knew it could spread to their back door next.

Annie was a firm believer in being prepared. The Foreign Mission Board had given her letters from Lottie Moon and other China missionaries about the workings of the Gospel Mission members. They had the best firsthand knowledge since this movement started among North China missionaries, headed by Martha Crawford's husband. Annie read the letters aloud. They could take no action to stop the movement, but Annie wanted the state leaders to be better informed. As she always told her followers, "Knowledge is power, interest, and inspiration."

The bold move Annie made at the Annual Meeting did not stop the Gospel Mission movement from finding sympathy in Georgia, however. Mrs. Stainback Wilson, a well-known and respected WMU leader in the state, was fast becoming a devoted follower of the Gospel Mission philosophy. More trouble was brewing, Annie knew, but she could not devote herself solely to solving that problem. She was beleaguered in many ways as 1894 progressed, personally as well as professionally. Mary Armstrong, the guiding star of Annie's life, was declining physically. Now Annie had her mother's health problems to worry about as well as her demanding WMU duties.

Mary had taught her children to lean on the Lord. Annie had spiritual resources, but nothing could completely take away the pain that Annie, like so many adult children before and after her, have felt. She had to watch her mother grow old. She had to come to the realization that even mothers don't live forever.

When she wasn't coping with personal issues, Annie was busy the summer of 1894 trying to help wipe out the Foreign Mission Board debt of $30,000. WMU agreed to raise $5,000 of that amount by August. Each state was assigned a goal and each woman church member, whether she belonged to WMU or not, was asked to give $1.00. With this approach, WMU raised $5,397 for the Foreign Mission Board.

At the Annual Meeting the women elected Fannie Heck's successor, Mrs. Abby Manly Gwathmey. She was very different from the young, never-married, affluent Fannie Heck. Mrs. Gwathmey was the widowed mother of nine children, with a rare Baptist pedigree. Her father, Basil Manly Sr., had been president of the University of Alabama; and her brother, Basil Jr., had helped begin the

Southern Baptist Theological Seminary. Another brother, Charles, served as president of Furman University.

Her family lineage, however, did not endow Mrs. Gwathmey with earthly riches. Her husband, a doctor who volunteered much time to the Foreign Mission Board as recording secretary, left her practically no money when he died. She could not pay her own travel expenses as Martha McIntosh and Fannie Heck had done. Though living close by in Richmond, she would not be able to travel often to Baltimore to meet with Annie. This suited Annie just fine. While she respected and admired Mrs. Gwathmey, she was satisfied to have inactive presidents who did not get in her way.

Baltimore, Winter 1895

"Martha McIntosh is married!" The news traveled like quicksilver through WMU circles. The first president of WMU, SBC, had become a bride at age 47. But it was who she married that floored Annie. Martha McIntosh was now Mrs. T. P. Bell, and stepmother to his children. Annie, once she digested the news, was happy for the couple, but . . . "They didn't even invite me to the wedding," she thought. Annie found this hurt her feelings, and, as usual, she was not one to keep hurt feelings to herself.

But Annie had more things on her mind than social slights. Things weren't going so well at the Home Mission Board either. At the last Annual Meeting WMU had voted to observe a week of self-denial, but with no date or specific object planned. When Dr. Tichenor revealed that the Home Mission Board might have to lay off missionaries due to Board indebtedness, the women had their purpose. The third week in March 1895 was set aside as a week of self-denial and prayer for the Home Mission Board. The HMB had also asked for $5,000. As they did for the Foreign Mission Board, the women raised more than that amount.

Annie read Baptist newspapers hungrily, though she could not take time out to read as thoroughly as she would have liked. She also read the state WMU papers, and was dismayed when she saw Mrs. Wilson and her sister, Mrs. C. E. Kerr, pushing Gospel Mission views through the Georgia WMU paper, *Our Mission Helper.*

"Why not ask the manager of the paper not to support the views of Mrs. Wilson and her sister?" one woman suggested when the topic was brought up.

"Because the manager of the paper *is* Mrs. Wilson's sister," someone answered.

"Oh dear."

Annie could not leave matters at a simple "Oh dear." She had to do something, or stand by and watch missions funds siphoned from the SBC mission boards and given to individual "faith" missionaries. The SBC boards and the Georgia state board opposed the Gospel Mission movement. Annie prayed hard for guidance and then asked the Board secretaries for advice. They put their heads together with Georgia secretary John B. Gibson.

Meanwhile, Mrs. Wilson got wind of their talks. She let it be known that this was Georgia state business, and that Annie should not interfere. Annie was asked to attend the Georgia state WMU meeting, but declined. It might make the situation more volatile if she attended, several of her counselors felt. She watched carefully and saw that the Georgia Central Committee was handling the situation well. Mary Emily Wright, Georgia's vice-president to WMU, SBC, had no sympathy for the independent movement, and led the central committee to force Mrs. Wilson's hand. Eventually she, her sister, and six other women resigned and formed a new organization which wanted to work with both the Southern Baptist mission boards and the Gospel Mission.

With the support of the Georgia Central Committee, the Georgia state board, and the Home Mission Board, Annie cut off Mrs. Wilson's organization from WMU the best way she knew how. She stopped sending them literature.

Washington, May 1895

"Oh, Dr. Whitsitt!" Annie called. "A word with you!" William Heth Whitsitt, the new president of Southern Baptist Theological Seminary, stopped to speak to Annie. He soon found out that no one ever had just one word with the WMU corresponding secretary.

Annie poured into Whitsitt's ear all she could about the work of WMU. She offered to keep him informed about the auxiliary's ongoing efforts. She had long hoped to encourage the seminary to promote WMU work with its students, who were the future pastors of the Convention. She felt it imperative to gain pastoral support. So far, her efforts to get professors to talk about the women's work had been unsuccessful, even though one of the professors, Franklin H. Kerfoot, had been her pastor. The Southern Baptist Convention was her golden opportunity to gain the attention of the new president. To her joy, he promised to promote the work at the seminary.

She was also thrilled at the WMU Annual Meeting to report that another of her efforts was bearing fruit. Annie had long coveted the District of Columbia for Southern Baptists, but its support had been split between North and South. She had convinced the women to form their foreign mission society into an organization that supported home and foreign missions work among Northern and Southern Baptists. She had visited several times, and had arranged for Marie Buhlmaier to work with German immigrants one day a week in Washington. That way the women could see for themselves the reality of Southern Baptist home missions. She had also shown the WMU committee hospitality by inviting them to visit her in Baltimore, where, of course, they could partake of meetings and see the work being done.

It had all been worth it. At this Annual Meeting, she proudly announced the District of Columbia's financial contributions to Southern Baptist missions causes.

Annie had come to Washington fearful that the dreaded Gospel Mission movement leaders would put in an appearance. More than once she checked the letters from missionaries which she had read before. She was prepared to read them aloud to the whole meeting if necessary. She breathed a sigh of relief when the meeting concluded and Mrs. Stainback Wilson and company had not caused trouble.

Someone who did make a reappearance, however, was the former president, Fannie Heck. She had regained her health and, being ready to serve, was voted back into office. Dear Mrs. Gwathmey had put her heart into the work, but, alas, no other part of her. Annie had no objection to Fannie Heck's election.

As Annie left for Baltimore, all was not roses and sunshine, however. While the Annual Meeting had been wonderful, she had had a falling out with Lansing Burrows, who had been the Convention recording secretary since 1881. The man with little eyeglasses and large mutton-chop whiskers was known for getting Convention minutes into the hands of delegates right after the meeting was over. This promptness made him very popular, but Annie felt only disdain for what she saw as an effort to grab glory with rushed and careless work.

This year, she and Brother Burrows exchanged heated words, and Annie went home offended. He certainly did not know how to treat a lady, and she resolved not to tolerate his boorish behavior.

Baltimore, Summer 1895

Annie would not let the situation with Lansing Burrows die. She complained to Dr. Frost of the recording secretary's rude treatment. Soon thereafter she received what she thought was only a halfhearted apology from Burrows, an apology which she felt sure had been wrung from him by Dr. Frost, who was trying to make peace between them.

As the summer marched on, Annie tried to shove thoughts of Lansing Burrows aside and plan her vacation. She hated the way work piled up when she was gone, but this year work would have to take second place. She and Alice were taking their mother to Groton, Connecticut.

"Why so far away?" friends asked.

"We have been told the sea air will do Mother good," Alice told them. Many people did go to the shore to regain their health, but the cure did not work for Mary. She grew progressively weaker. Annie fussed and worried over all she should have been doing in Baltimore. It was a relief to go home. No one had told Annie that the sea air would aggravate her neuralgia as it did. That was one "cure" she was in no hurry to take again.

That summer was useful in one way. Annie had found time to write all the women missionaries to explain the work of WMU. Many of the missionaries wrote back, and she shared the letters with others, feeling everyone should have keen interest and sympathy toward the people she called "our substitutes."

Baltimore, Late 1895

Annie pushed on with her many interests. She kept up with the conflict at Southern Seminary. Dr. Whitsitt had kept his word about supporting WMU at the seminary, and taken many steps to acquaint students with the organization and what it did for missions. She corresponded with him, suggesting speakers who would come—but not at WMU expense—to talk about the organization.

Later in the year she traveled to Atlanta to address a Woman's Congress on the topic "Woman's Work in the Evangelization of the Homes of the Colored People."

Mary G. Burdette, Annie's counterpart with the northern Woman's Home Mission Society, was also scheduled to speak and the women feared she would mention social equality between blacks and whites. This was typical of the tension between Northern and Southern Baptists, who had different methods but the same desire to work with the black population. Annie prepared her remarks with the northern woman's possible comments in mind, though she did not think any problem would occur.

When the Baptist Young People's Union (BYPU) organized in Atlanta that November, Annie was very happy. She used her influence to shape the BYPU to have a missions emphasis.

Annie could not bear to see any opportunity slip by, and her work habits reflected her many interests and commitments. She started work at 7:00 A.M. and often worked until the middle of the night. She worked while plagued with headaches, neuralgia, and even the flu. As she gained experience, she learned that sometimes an idea would take flight quicker if she would suggest it to someone else and then let them take credit for it. What difference did it make to her, as long as God's kingdom was furthered?

WMU's influence grew, and with it, so did the many bids for Annie's time. She was buried under a mountain of requests for help, advice, and attention. She still worked hard in her church and in the Maryland Mission Rooms. Her mother needed her more than ever; Alice could not do everything at home. She, too, had her calling from God with her writing.

Annie did not know how much the strain of her work was showing. At the Annual Meeting, it had been Fannie Heck's turn to notice how tense and tired Annie looked. She wanted to get Annie more help. This was difficult, though, since Annie refused a salary and thought as many people as possible around her should also forego payment for their work. Annie had been known to say, "Rewards await us yonder, work awaits us here." She possibly didn't realize that people not financially independent had to have a few rewards—in the form of a salary—while still on earth.

Late 1896

Where had the year gone? Annie wondered as she looked back through her notebooks and correspondence. She had been busy and for the most part, happy, though there had been some conflicts brewing. T. P. Bell had left the Sunday School Board to become editor of the *Christian Index* in Georgia and dear Dr. Frost had replaced him at the Board. Annie had spent time collecting names for mailing lists, writing curriculum, and corresponding with Dr. Frost about many things—Bible distribution, boxes to Sunday School missionaries, using frontier missionaries as colporteurs, literature for missionaries, Missionary Day in Sunday School, and a host of other work.

The Foreign Mission Board was still in debt, and it weighed on Annie as if it were her own personal problem. More than once, she thought of just going into business for herself and using her profits to support missions work. Annie felt, justifiably so, that she could have been a success in business. Other women were beginning to make their mark in the business world. But she, Annie, would have been making money for a different reason—not for greed or to compete with men, but to serve God.

She quickly exited these castles in the sky, however, and came down to earth. She had enough to do already, with writing and speaking and helping organize missions work. The black women (Annie liked to think of them as "brunettes") were growing in their desire to organize for missions. Just this year National Baptist leader L. G. Jordan had visited with her to discuss organization. Annie practically jumped at the chance. Not only would it develop the powers of black women at home, it would mean more black missionaries someday. Annie could envision a day when black American missionaries took the gospel to Africa. As a first step, Annie agreed to write material for the *Afro-American Herald.*

And there were the Sunbeam Bands, a missions education organization for children. George Braxton Taylor, who had founded Sunbeam Band work with children several years earlier, resigned from it and gave the work to the Foreign Mission Board (FMB; now International Mission Board). Taylor's uncle had been the first corresponding secretary of the FMB, and it was natural that his nephew think first of the Board. The FMB, however, could not wait to ask WMU to accept the work, which it did.

Of course, Annie thought as she leafed through her notebooks, not everything was handed to WMU. Take the Italian work in Baltimore, for instance. John Eager, missionary to Italy, was in Baltimore during the summer. He often preached at Eutaw Place. Annie had approached him about starting a work with the Italian immigrants that thronged the city.

"But, Miss Annie, I am going back to Italy soon!" he protested. Well, she told him, what difference did that make? He could begin the work and someone else could then keep it alive. For her part, she would ask the Home Mission Board for funds, the Sunday School Board for literature and Bibles, and the BYPU for young volunteers. Which she did, and the work was begun.

As she had written to Dr. Frost, "I do recognize that our Heavenly Father has given me quickness to bring forces together." She enjoyed this, she told him, as long as it was "such work as I am capable of without assuming responsibility." She had quite enough responsibility without looking for more. She was always fighting one battle or another. Women were constantly wanting to designate gifts instead of give their money to the mission boards wholeheartedly. People nitpicked about the missionary boxes. There were what she saw as constant intrusions into Southern Baptist areas by Northern Baptists.

Annie was not discouraged. She turned to her well-worn Bible and read the passages that gave her the most comfort. "Fear thou not; for I am with thee: be not dismayed; for I am thy God: I will strengthen thee; yea, I will uphold thee with the right hand of my righteousness" (Isa. 41:10). "As thy days, so shall thy strength be" (Deut. 33:25). And of course, her personal motto, Go Forward. If it was good enough for Moses when he guided the children of Israel, it was good enough for her.

Baltimore, 1897

Annie took some time from other work to write to her friends at the Foreign Mission Board. "I am more and more persuaded that all that is required of those who have the work in charge is faithful seed sowing. The harvest is bound to follow.

"No matter how heavy the burden, daily strength is given, so I expect we need not give ourselves any concern as to what the outcome will be, but think 'go forward.'"

The burdens were getting heavier, although the joys grew as well. She had just met a most remarkable young "brunette" woman, Nannie Helen Burroughs, who was intelligent, deeply visionary, and dripping with leadership potential. She, L. G. Jordan, Miss Burroughs, two of Annie's Executive Committee members, and a black Baltimore pastor spent four hours one frigid January day preparing for a constitution for the National Baptist women's missions organization. They laid other plans as well. At the next convention, leaders would call on the women to organize. In the meantime, they would all work together—with Annie in the background—to stir interest in missions among both black women and their pastors. Miss Burroughs would take the lead in organizing the women in societies so they would be ready to seize the moment when national organization was called for.

When she wasn't working with the black women, Annie was coming up with new ideas for making Southern

Baptists stronger. "What about an almanac?" She could see it clearly in her mind: brief historical sketches of the boards, important facts, encouraging statistics of Southern Baptist growth. She wrote to Dr. Frost about the idea. She would even be the editor, if he liked. After all, she had the time.

Dr. Frost liked the idea; the Northern Baptists did not. Their publishing arm already printed materials about Southern Baptists. With the yearbook, what need was there for an almanac? Annie, however, did not want Southern Baptists to be dependent on Northern Baptists for information about their own denomination. Annie's protective streak came out again; she still feared Northern Baptists would overwhelm Southern Baptists. After all, were they not still coming south of the Mason-Dixon Line to work with blacks? Mary Burdette had even met with Annie and complained that Northern missionaries who came south were treated rudely, and that their work should be supported.

The Northern Baptists could not stop the almanac, but to Annie's displeasure, Dr. Frost chose Lansing Burrows to be the editor. Usually she didn't mind conceiving an idea and letting someone else be in charge but . . . Lansing Burrows! Annie would have to work with him. She was going to compile many of the statistics for the almanac. But, she didn't have to put up with rudeness, and she *would* not. From his reactions, Brother Burrows was as pleased to work with her as she was with him. He found her unwillingness to rush things irritating. They did get the work done, however.

Then there was the matter of the week of self-denial in March. She had tried to have the week observed as widely as possible. But this year, a Virginia church had objected to it on the grounds that it was unscriptural, led to covetousness, and decreased receipts of the Home Mission Board. They drafted a resolution to that effect.

"How can self-denial be unscriptural?" Annie cried to no one in particular when she read the resolution. Was the church even talking about the same thing she had been promoting, which was meant to benefit the Home Mission Board? As she investigated, Annie became suspicious that the problem lay with the pastor, F. C. McConnell, who had once been at the Home Mission Board.

"I find him not overburdened with discretion," Annie stated dryly when she explained her suspicions to others. She worried that he would bring up the matter at the Convention. If so, T. T. Eaton, the editor of the *Western Recorder* and nemesis of WMU, would jump on the subject.

Wilmington, May 1897

"The week of self-denial in March has been approved." The women had voted at Annual Meeting that criticism or no, they would proceed with the week of self-denial in March to benefit the Home Mission Board. Easily decided, that topic paled in comparison to the battle being waged over the Sunday School recommendations.

Annie wanted the recommendation passed, which referred to WMU's support of the Sunday School Board Bible Fund. The Board wanted WMU's great fund-raising power to benefit their Bible Fund. Earlier, there had been an amount mentioned, but the final resolution only asked for WMU's "cooperation." To Annie, this was a natural outgrowth of WMU work. To Fannie Heck, it was not.

The president put up quite an argument against being involved with the Sunday School Board in such a manner. With her polished voice, expressive hands, and face, Fannie Heck made a very charismatic leader. But then there was Annie, tall, commanding, and confident. The women approved the recommendation.

Baltimore, Late 1897

Annie delighted in reading the reports from the National Baptist Convention in September. Things were going well. By December, however, L. G. Jordan had to report a split in the work. There was friction between Northern and Southern Baptists. Annie fired off several letters to the American Baptist Publication Society about the issue; it was interfering with the black churches getting on with the work of organizing for missions.

With all her work in WMU, Annie was still directing the work of the Maryland Mission Rooms. A near catastrophe had occurred in late November when a fire raged across the street from the rooms, burning down a store and killing a woman. Baltimore had had several bad fires during the years. Annie knew, although she was not old enough at the time to remember, that her own father's business holdings had been severely damaged by fire. She thanked God the mission rooms were still intact as she faced the uncertainties ahead in 1898.

Baltimore, 1898

Annie was determined to do all she could to promote the Sunday School Board recommendation. Literature had been printed promoting the fund. She noticed none was ordered from North Carolina, Miss Heck's home state.

Annie was beginning to change her mind about Fannie Heck. The woman was opinionated, one might even say stubborn, and wanted to have too much of a hand in the affairs of WMU, SBC. If Annie saw any irony in having a president in some ways so much like herself, she kept quiet about it.

To Annie's understanding, the president's job was to preside at the Annual Meeting, and, when in Baltimore, at the Executive Committee meeting. Since Annie had helped draft the constitution, she felt she knew more about the president's role than did Fannie Heck. It would all come to a head soon. On January 25, there would be a called WMU Executive Committee meeting. Today, January 24, Miss Heck was coming to speak with her on the subject.

Fannie Heck arrived and the two strong-willed women were soon in an argument.

"You have used your power to push the Sunday School Board on us. You have interpreted the recommendation of the annual meeting to mean money, when it clearly means simply influence and promotion," Fannie charged. Annie refused to be intimidated.

"On the contrary, 'co-operation' means contributions as well as promotion and I have interpreted the action correctly," she declared.

Annie was wounded by Fannie Heck's words. She was saying that Annie had used her position to force her own will on WMU, SBC. Drawing on her dignity to sustain her, Annie offered Fannie Heck the option of bringing up the matter at the next day's meeting, or at Annual Meeting, if she wished. Then she would have an opportunity to refute the charges.

"I'm not falling into that trap," thought the president. "This is a private matter between us. I see no reason to bring it up publicly," she said. And she did not. Emboldened by the president's silence, Annie decided that Fannie Heck probably wouldn't bring up the matter again. Just to be on the safe side, however, she wrote Dr. Frost and suggested he not change the wording of the recommendation.

But then, later the president did make mention of the recommendation again. This was a sign to Annie that the fight would continue. What should she do? She did what she always tended to do, seek out a trusted man's advice. Annie wrote to Judge Jonathan Haralson for his opinion on what the recommendation meant. His opinion should certainly be worth something. Not only was he a member of the Alabama Supreme Court, he was president of the Southern Baptist Convention.

Annie's unease deepened when she found out Fannie Heck had visited Dr. Willingham in Richmond after the fight with Annie in Baltimore. Of course she had the right to visit Dr. Willingham, but what if she were seeking *his* advice?

Whatever the two discussed, the Foreign Mission Board secretary tried to stay on good terms with both women, hoping earnestly they could work out their differences so that WMU would not be damaged by the conflict. Annie was sustained by the letter from Judge Haralson, who sided with her interpretation.

Until the Annual Meeting, Annie stewed over the situation and wrote letters to Dr. Frost. She advised him not to write to Fannie Heck unless she saw the letter first. She even suggested she might not continue as corresponding secretary.

For her part, the president knew Annie was trying to influence Dr. Frost. She also felt Annie had worked on the Maryland vice-president of WMU, SBC. At the Annual Meeting and the Executive Committee meeting, Fannie Heck made no mention of the Sunday School Board recommendation. All Annie's strategies in case of a showdown were for nothing. The recommendation passed. The strain between the two leaders was obvious, however. The showdown, as in the popular dime novels about the Wild West, was still coming.

It came just a few days later, in the form of a letter from Fannie Heck, reminding Annie she would not often be in the Executive Committee meetings. She wanted meeting agendas sent to her ahead of time so she could write her opinions in time for the committee to have them.

Annie refused. The bylaws clearly stated that in the absence of the president, the vice-president of the state in which the committee met would preside. This was the Maryland vice-president, a personal friend of Annie's. In her refusal, Annie pointed out that since the work of WMU was based on the boards' recommendations, and Fannie Heck knew those recommendations, she could write her opinion any time she pleased.

Fannie Heck was stunned by this answer. It was obvious to her that Annie had had the run of things for far too long, and had no respect for the president. She wrote to

Dr. Willingham for advice. To his credit, instead of telling both women to leave him alone because he had a mission board to run, he tried to be a peacemaker without taking sides.

The president decided to take a stand. It was not just because of the way Annie was treating her personally; this conflict would determine the future of WMU. Either the elected president was the leader of WMU, or she was a useless figurehead. Fannie Heck had no intention of being a figurehead.

But, she was a sensitive woman, too. She had no desire to cause personal divisions and ill feelings by having the showdown at an Annual Meeting. Although she would be outnumbered at the Executive Committee meeting, that was where she intended to make her feelings known. She had consulted with Martha McIntosh Bell, who did not agree with Annie's interpretation of the constitution.

"To delay would be cowardly," she told herself. If only some kind friend would let Miss Armstrong know she was in the wrong. Was any such friend available? Fannie Heck did not see one, no matter how hard she looked.

As for Annie, she wrote Dr. Frost that she hoped he would take her side, since it was for the Sunday School Board's sake she had originally gotten into this dispute. But she knew she was right. "I do not propose to yield one iota," she wrote.

The president notified the Executive Committee that she would be bringing up the matter at the June meeting. Annie did not get a copy of the letter; of course, Alice did, which was as good as Annie receiving one. Annie's letter from the president just let her know that she wanted the role of the president interpreted.

The June meeting came, but Fannie Heck did not attend. Annie had Judge Haralson's letters from the previous dispute. The committee, at Alice's suggestion, tabled the matter until Judge Haralson could render another opinion. Annie then went into action. Dr. Tichenor came to Baltimore to discuss the matter with her. "Miss Heck is acting so strangely!" Annie told him. She then flooded the Board secretaries with copies of letters, the WMU constitution, and the bylaws. She sent Haralson volumes as well, and asked his advice.

Then Fannie Heck wrote and asked for his advice.

Finally, the coveted advice came. In his expert opinion, Judge Haralson found that it was not incumbent on the corresponding secretary to give the president an agenda, though it would be courteous to do so. As for the vice-president taking the president's role, that simply meant presiding over the meeting, not making presidential decisions.

Both women sobered as they read the rest of the judge's letter. He chided them for the conflict. It was "embarrassing" and "not about the weightier matters of the law." He urged them to just let it go. But they could not, or would not.

Montgomery, July 1898

Three men sat in a room, miserable in the sweltering Alabama heat. They were equally uncomfortable with what they had to discuss. Dr. Tichenor, Dr. Frost, and Dr. Willingham were talking about what to do with Annie Armstrong and Fannie Heck. Their feud had the potential to damage all the good that WMU had accomplished in the last decade. It was finally decided to write both women, asking them to come for a conference with them and Judge Haralson.

Annie fumed when she read the letter. They were putting her in the same category as Fannie Heck! But Annie was in the right! Very well, she answered, she would come. But could they please have the conference close to her home, perhaps Washington? She never left her mother for long anymore. Annie hoped the men intended to judge correctly instead of whitewashing things.

"I think I do see that God's hand is guiding in the way he is showing some of us what ought to be done under existing circumstances, but I fail entirely to see any signs of God's hand in what has occurred. I trust he will over-rule it for good," she wrote Frost. Annie, always depen-dent on the Holy Spirit for guidance, voiced a fervent hope that divine guidance would be given.

Fannie Heck answered that she would come, but asked for the conference to be held in September. She felt this was an official, not a personal matter. She had no new argu-ments to offer. However, she cautioned that the secretaries should bear the responsibility for whatever happened.

Norfolk, Late August 1898

The conference was convened. All parties discussed the mat-ter. It was basically a peace summit between the two women. Fannie Heck, tired and still not completely well, offered to decline reelection the following year, something she had already decided before the conference. Annie agreed not to discuss the matter, even with the Executive Committee.

After the conference, Dr. Willingham wrote the Execu-tive Committee and said the conference had been "full and free." Fannie Heck would not seek reelection.

Annie should have left the conference elated. She had won. But the end of the conference was the beginning of a great deal of soul searching for her. The question, Is it time for me to step aside? Let others do things differently? would haunt her for months to come.

8
Growing Pains

Baltimore, Late 1898

Annie raced through the row house, holding her long skirts so they would not trip her as she ran. The household was in an uproar. Mary Armstrong had taken a bad fall. When Annie reached her mother, she was appalled to see a terrible cut on her mother's head that had bled profusely. Mary had also wrenched her back when she fell. The doctor was called and tended to the cut and Mary was put to bed. Things settled down.

Her daughters' nerves did not settle down as quickly. Always a dainty woman, Mary was frail in her old age. Not only was it hard to see their beloved mother bleeding and in pain, but it was another sign to Annie, Mamie, and Alice that their mother was no longer the tower of strength who had cared for them through civil war and family tragedies. The daughters had become the protectors and caregivers for the mother, and they were learning that was never an easy transition.

Meanwhile, the peace conference had only partly solved the tension between Annie and Fannie Heck. The president found subtle ways to get back at Annie. For her part, she would extend no olive branch to Fannie Heck.

A letter finally reached Annie in September, letting her know that North Carolina WMU would not send out the names of Sunday School missionaries as possible box recipients. Only Home Mission Board missionaries would get boxes from North Carolina societies. This was Fannie Heck's way of letting Annie know she had not changed her mind about WMU support for the Sunday School Board.

As irritating as this was, Annie tried to stay silent. She had given her word in Norfolk not to discuss these things with Executive Committee members.

Though she did not write Fannie Heck, Annie kept up her flood of letters to the Board secretaries and WMU leaders. She urged the Board leaders to talk about WMU at state conventions. She wanted pastors to get a positive impression of what WMU could do for them. Annie prayed for God to send Southern Baptists mature pastors. She had always sought advice from experienced men of God, but the new crop of young pastors coming through Baltimore had so much to learn. "The boys' brigade," Annie sometimes called them. Her other favorite nickname for them was the "juveniles."

In order to help get out the word, Annie came up with a plan to have WMU work reported in district associational meetings. She also urged on WMU leaders and members to make the most of all opportunities open to them. In one report she sent words of encouragement: "Let us not be weary in well doing, but accepting from God each new day as a new opportunity, resolve there shall be no squandered hours, no wasted minutes." As the standard of living rose in the country and for Southern Baptists, women found themselves with more opportunities for travel and education, more leisure time. Annie wanted those extra personal resources given to the Lord's work. She could not abide idle, self-indulgent women.

Baltimore, 1899

As soon as the new year came in, Annie started to worry that Fannie Heck would back out of the Norfolk agreement.

"If Fannie Heck stays, I go," she vowed privately. When word reached her that the president planned to be at the Annual Meeting in Louisville, she refused to go herself. As strong as Annie was, conflict and confrontation wore on her nerves, and she wanted to avoid it with Fannie Heck.

On March 6 the post delivered Annie a letter from Fannie Heck. Reading it, Annie saw it was really a letter for the Executive Committee. She was telling them she had decided not to accept reelection.

Annie relaxed as the import of the letter sank in. Fannie Heck had kept her word. Suddenly, Annie thought the Louisville meeting looked much more attractive. She sat down and quickly wrote back to Fannie Heck about closing out the year's accounts and arranging the Annual Meeting. Then, she invited her niece, May, and one of cousin Joshua Levering's daughters to go with her. Mamie, bless her, would stay in Baltimore and help with their mother.

Louisville, May 1899

Fannie Heck had never responded to Annie's letter about arrangements for the meeting, but she presided ably. She was also beautiful in a gray dress and matching gray bonnet. She was noticeably distracted, however; she had brought her mother with her, and Mrs. Heck was ill. Like Annie, Fannie Heck was a loving and dutiful daughter.

She was also late to the meeting, which gave Jessie Stakely of Washington a chance to be presiding officer. She was not in the normal chain of succession to fill in for the president. It also did not occur to most of the delegates that perhaps the president's tardiness was on purpose so that Mrs. Stakely could take center stage. To most delegates, Fannie Heck would have been late because her mother was ill. If her tardiness was for any other reason, Fannie Heck kept it to herself.

Many of the women wanted Mary Oldham Eagle, the wife of the governor of Arkansas, and one of the women messengers, booted out of the Southern Baptist Convention several years earlier. Annie wanted Jessie Stakely. She had been in the Stakely home many times when business took her to Washington. Jessie Stakely's husband, who pastored First Baptist Church, was prominent as an excellent preacher and brilliant man. His lovely gray-eyed wife was also respected, the product of three generations of Baptist preacher families.

When nominations came the names of Jessie Stakely and Mary Emily Wright, Georgia WMU president, were offered for president. Miss Wright promptly withdrew her name, and Sarah Jessie Davis Stakely succeeded Fannie Heck.

Annie beamed as Mrs. Stakely was voted into office. She had known the woman for several years, and knew her efforts in strengthening WMU work in the District of Columbia. Mrs. Stakely's connection with First Baptist Church, plus her own good qualities, would surely cement bonds between the District and Southern Baptists.

Then, Fannie Heck caused Annie one last bit of distress. As she was giving Mrs. Stakely advice about her new office she said, "As president I often send missionary letters to the state Baptist papers." Annie kept quiet, though she wanted to say, "That's *my* job, not the president's." There would be time enough to deal with that later, though. Now the meeting was over, Fannie Heck was gone, and Annie wanted to get home to her mother.

Later, after writing to Dr. Willingham for advice, Annie wrote a polite note to Mrs. Stakely, saying that since the president had a family to care for, Annie would send missionary letters to the state papers, relieving the president of that chore. It was just as well, for not long after becoming president Mrs. Stakely became gravely ill and was admitted to Johns Hopkins Hospital. She recovered, and became a respected leader among the women and an equal to Annie.

Baltimore, Fall 1899

Franklin Kerfoot, Annie's pastor from 1877 to 1882, had left his post at Southern Seminary to take Dr. Tichenor's place at the Home Mission Board. Annie could not have been more pleased; she thought the world of him.

Dr. Kerfoot returned the favor by speaking well of WMU and Annie to his seminary students. How would he describe Annie? He was diplomatic but forthright. "She has a will as imperious as Julius Caesar's," he said. He hastened to say, "Yet as her pastor, I found her always in the way of the Lord's mind." Kerfoot wanted to further assure the future pastors that WMU women were not pushing for the right to vote or wear bloomers. "These women are not undertaking to run anything nor to get out of their spheres; they are the most womanly women I have ever known."

He did not know that the woman he was praising had been told by her doctors that she needed to rest for several months. All the late hours and extensive travel had taken its toll. Annie had not even gone for the usual summer vacation for several years, not since the disastrous seaside trip in 1895. She could not leave her mother, and Mary Armstrong was failing fast. Finally this amazing woman who had been mother, teacher, guide, advisor, and friend to her daughters, passed way on November 15.

Mamie was grief-stricken, but Alice and Annie were completely at a loss. Mamie had not lived with their mother for several years. She had a husband and children. At age 49, Annie had always lived under her mother's roof. She and Alice knew no other life.

After they buried their mother, the two sisters discussed the future. They could board somewhere and get out from under the burden of running a residence. Freedom was attractive but . . . the row house had been home for 36 years. They would stay on McCulloh Street.

Baltimore, Early 1900

Annie eagerly awaited the new year. The last few years had been painful, and she wanted to put that pain behind her. She chose to start the new year and the new century by focusing on all the good that had taken place. The women were better organized and better trained, and were hungry for new projects and more missions information.

Yet, it was time to go forward, not to rest. She wrote in her report, "As pioneers of the 20th Century, we face responsibilities for helping to lay a foundation for far *greater work* than was possible by Southern Baptists in the past. With hearty enthusiasm, let us follow our divine leader, and by unity of plans, by systematic, proportionate giving, and by personal activity, 'Ring out the old, old story, Ring in Thy Kingdom Come.'"

Annie's strength was not up to all the plans she had, but she would not take a vacation. She had promised Dr. Kerfoot she would help with the New Century Movement. He had been made chair of the committee overseeing this plan even before he was Home Mission Board secretary. It was a goal of the Southern Baptist Convention to go into the twentieth century with more missions giving, more mission societies, and more churches using Southern Baptist literature. The ultimate goal of the campaign was to reach churches that were not giving anything to missions.

When Dr. Kerfoot had first asked Annie for her help, she agreed to give it, but with conditions. First, he had to give her direction. She would not take personal responsibility for what was done. Second, she wanted the boards to pay for another typewriter and clerk, but the expense would not be considered a WMU expense.

At the 1900 Annual Meeting, Annie used her influence to get the women to agree to "cooperate" with the New Century Movement. The Southern Baptist Convention, meanwhile, created a Committee on Cooperation, also chaired by Dr. Kerfoot. This committee would devise the New Century plans.

Annie turned her attention in April to foreign missions. She accompanied a number of Southern Baptist leaders to New York for the Ecumenical Conference on Foreign Missions. Though decidedly not ecumenical in most of her work, Annie found the conference and its delegates fascinating. She met people from all over the world, who showed her many new ways of thinking about foreign missions. Anything that could stimulate her thinking and help her be more innovative pleased Annie.

Baltimore, Summer 1900

"Hello, Miss Annie." The man greeting her had an open face with large eyes and a strong chin. His mustache connected to the mutton whiskers and sideburns that covered his square jaw.

"Dr. Kerfoot, how good to see you," Annie replied. He had wasted no time in visiting Annie to discuss how much help WMU, SBC, would give the New Century Movement.

Their meeting was cordial, since they were old friends, but Annie refused to commit WMU to anything more specific than cooperation. She had learned a few things in her years as corresponding secretary. She remembered how quickly criticism of WMU came any time it stepped out of its women-only sphere.

Annie would work herself into the ground, but WMU must be protected. As she and Dr. Kerfoot chatted, she asked question after question. Who would be in charge of what part of the movement? What did the committee have planned? She soon saw that little had been planned. She explained to Dr. Kerfoot that she could envision months, even years, of work to reach the committee's stated goals.

"The state Baptist convention secretaries will meet this month," he said. "Why not attend the meeting so you may hear the discussion?"

Annie demurred, but later wrote Dr. Willingham and Dr. Frost for their advice. Dr. Willingham, the veteran of hundreds of meetings, advised against going until the committee had made plans. Dr. Frost advised the opposite: go and get in on the beginning of things. Annie looked at the letters from her two trusted advisors, advising two completely different things. Now what to do? She compromised by suggesting she and Mrs. Stakely both attend the committee meeting in August. Dr. Kerfoot liked the idea, so on August 2 she and Mrs. Stakely joined the committee at Old Point Comfort, Virginia.

The men lost no time in trying to recruit their help. "We ask that WMU, SBC, use its influence to encourage people to give to Southern Baptist causes and use Southern Baptist literature." These were both goals close to Annie's heart; surely no one could criticize WMU in those efforts.

The next request was completely in WMU's area of work, to encourage more churches to start mission societies. Annie and Mrs. Stakely agreed to that request, and said they would encourage the women to help their pastors with a New Century meeting in each church.

As soon as Annie returned to Baltimore she started sending out letters to societies about the plans. While she wanted to support all the goals, she was most determined to pursue enlargement, the starting of more societies. In some states, only one-tenth of churches had mission societies. Even Virginia, the cornerstone of missions giving, could boast of societies in half its churches.

"There is only one way to start this many societies," Annie told herself. "The personal touch is needed."

Annie planned out the traveling that would take her throughout the Convention. At the same time, she started contacting churches. This was part of what she had promised Dr. Kerfoot back when she asked for the clerk and typewriter. She combined lists of churches and church clerks with schedules of district associational meetings.

She sent state WMU leaders the lists for their state with instructions to encourage the New Century Movement. Then she sent literature that would help the women help their pastors conduct New Century meetings.

Annie herself surveyed pastors to find out which churches did not have societies. Then she followed up with contacts with key women in those churches. She worked hour after hour on the project, doing tedious work, compiling facts and figures, toiling away for no salary. The work was what mattered.

As much as the New Century Movement consumed her time, Annie found another new project for the new century. She wanted to resurrect the Church Building Loan Fund at the Home Mission Board. It had died several years earlier when some people feared that raising money for a loan fund would overwhelm other missions work.

Annie did not think it would. She had seen the frontier churches; she knew how much they needed help. When an anonymous donor gave the Woman's Baptist Home Mission Society of Maryland $1,000 to be given to the Home Mission Board for just such a cause, Annie saw her opportunity. She convinced Baptist women to give $3,500 more dollars to the fund, and urged the states to donate $1,000 each. The whole time, she exhorted and cajoled the Home Mission Board to restart the fund. Because of Annie, it finally did.

Baltimore and Richmond and Parts Out West, August–September 1900

"Alice, I am definitely going." Annie focused her most determined look on her older sister, and found her immune to the gaze which had made others tremble.

"Consider the benefits of the trip. I will gain personal knowledge of the frontier field. I will be in Indian Territory when the two conventions there consolidate. I will be able to present New Century plans to the state WMU central committees on the way to and from Oklahoma. It's only 4,000 miles."

"I protest strenuously," Alice said firmly.

"I know," Annie said, and went on with her plans. She was going to Oklahoma and the Indian Territory. She would spend 40 days out West in August and September, traveling across the prairie and plains by train, wagon, or whatever other conveyance was to be had. To Annie it was a dream come true. To Alice, it was a nightmare. What was a well-bred eastern lady like Annie going to do in the wilds of Indian Territory? What if she met with an outlaw?

If Mrs. Stakely had somehow not convinced Annie to accept travel expenses from the boards, Annie would not have been going on the trip. She had taken neither salary nor expense money, but now she was willing to take funds if it would enhance her ability to support the frontier work and work with the Indians, who were still very important to Annie.

It helped that at the Annual Meeting at Hot Springs, the women voiced vigorous approval for the trip. They could see the benefit in it. The only thing Annie hated about the trip was the timing. The black Baptist women had invited her to their organizational meeting, and she would have loved to have been there for the historic event.

Though she had traveled a great deal, this was a new experience for Annie. She dogged Dr. Willingham with question after question about packing, schedules, expenses, and the physical difficulties of travel. She also had to do a great deal of work ahead of time so everything would be left in good order. She had literature printed ahead of time and shipped to the states. She made sure she had plenty of notebooks for recording impressions of the journey.

She also made plans with and for her traveling companion, Anna Schimp. Anna was a Swiss woman of good intellect and comfortable means. Her only weakness was her poor English; but her many strong points, such as a sense of humor and a dedication to missions, outweighed that.

On August 20 the two women set out. They stopped in Louisville and St. Louis to meet with the WMU central committees of those states. She spoke at a women's meeting in Louisville where she inspired the women with her dreams for the future. It was Missouri, though, that Annie was most eager to reach. The contributions from that border state were, in her words, "deplorably small." That, coupled with the support the state gave the Northern Baptists, concerned her greatly.

Finally the train reached Oklahoma and Indian Territory. The temperatures were nothing like Baltimore—it was not unusual to be over 100°F in the daytime, with cool nights. The strong sun blinded Annie, the dust choked her, the lack of trees shocked her. It was another world, but she was glad to be in it.

If the West was a new world to Annie, she was new to it also. More than once men stared at the six-foot-tall eastern woman who, before climbing on a horse, would put on a cameo brooch, some lace, and a bonnet. By carriage, train, and horseback, Annie visited little churches, missionaries, mining towns, Indian agencies, and women's meetings. She saw how much the churches struggled and how little they had.

After a hard day of organizing women's societies, Annie and Anna would retire, exhausted but excited by all the Lord was showing them. Sometimes they had lovely guest rooms in fine homes, or decent hotel rooms. Other accommodations were not so good. There was the time Annie found an unemptied slop jar in her room, and the time they had to put up a privacy screen when sharing a room with strangers. It was worth it all, though, to be among the missionaries, her substitutes on the frontier.

One of her main reasons for going out West was the consolidation of organization taking place. On September 7 she and Mary Burdette, corresponding secretary of the Northern Baptist Woman's Home Mission Society, were both at the general meeting in Durant, Oklahoma. The women would hold three meetings: one for those supporting the Northern work, one for those supporting Southern work, and one joint meeting.

Through the meeting Annie was tense with expectation. The decisions made at the meeting would affect the whole future of Southern Baptist work in this part of the country. The final result was that the women decided to form one organization with dual alignment. This was not what Annie had wanted, but perhaps it was the best she could hope for. Her greatest fear was that since Northern Baptists paid missionaries to organize the women's work, and Southern Baptists did not, the Northern Baptists would dominate.

"I will have to do the organizing," Annie told herself.

On the way home Annie made good use of her time, speaking to WMU central committees in several states. She also spoke at rallies and meetings as her train carried her through Texas, Arkansas, Tennessee, Alabama, Georgia, South Carolina, North Carolina, and Virginia. When she reached home, her neat notebooks showed that she had attended 59 meetings and made 39 addresses.

Everywhere she spoke she tried to impress on the women the needs of the frontier as well as the foreign missions needs in war-torn China. She reminded women of the power of prayer available to each of them.

"Whatever may be our circumstances in life," she said, "may each one of us really believe that by way of the Throne we have *unlimited power*. Would that we could realize that the success of missions and our prayers are linked together."

Baltimore, Late 1900

The Maryland Mission Rooms were becoming the victim of their own success. It was time for the operations to grow and expand. This had led to the question, How was this best to be done? Annie, with her keen vision, could imagine the Sunday School Board taking them over. She hoped that one day the Board would be the main publisher for Southern Baptists, and perhaps the Baltimore location could be a branch office.

Annie learned that the Maryland Baptist Union Association, which was the state convention, preferred to offer the rooms to the mission boards. Annie had rejected the first offer, which was for WMU to receive the rooms and all assets.

"WMU does not receive funds; it simply acts as an agent for Convention boards," she explained when she declined the offer. The association then offered the work to the boards, saying that WMU would be the agent in charge of the work. If the work was still too much of a burden, the boards would have the right to transfer the work to some other agency.

Though she still wanted to see the mission rooms go to the Sunday School Board, Annie obeyed the association's directive. She went to Richmond to speak with Dr. Willingham and his associate, Mr. E. E. Bomar, about the transfer. Then in December she wrote to both boards recapping the history of the mission rooms and offering them to the boards. "Why are they taking so long to decide?" she thought. Certainly they would take the mission rooms.

Baltimore, Early 1901

"I am astonished, grieved, and hurt," Annie wrote to Dr. Willingham. She had just learned the Foreign Mission Board had actually rejected the offer of the mission rooms! He wrote back, assuring her that he was also surprised by the Board's action. The Foreign Mission Board had suggested that the Sunday School Board would be better suited to having the mission rooms. Since this was what Annie had desired all along, people could not be blamed if they were puzzled at the offense she took at getting exactly what she had wanted.

The Home Mission Board accepted the offer. In February, Annie wrote to Dr. Frost about the transfer proposal. In April, Dr. Frost and Dr. Kerfoot arrived in Baltimore for the formal transfer of the rooms. It was agreed that Annie would continue managing them and that WMU would be the agent.

While all this was going on, Annie continued spreading the word about frontier work. She had gone to Valdosta for the Georgia WMU Annual Meeting. Mrs. Stakely, who now lived in Montgomery, Alabama, also attended. Annie poured out her heart to the women. She described the conditions in the mining camps, the hard work of the missionaries, and the good the New Century Movement would do.

"Would you support a missionary in Indian Territory?" she asked the women. Moved by her report, the women agreed. In April, the Virginia WMU board in Richmond was also persuaded to support a missionary in the area.

Annie was heartened by this, but something occurred in April that was only a foreshadow of much of her trouble in the future. T. P. Bell, whom she had so liked and admired, wrote a critical editorial in the *Christian Index*. He had already written one editorial back in 1899 questioning WMU's actions and methods. Now he accused WMU of caring more about home missions than it did foreign missions. He even went so far as to say that most of the missionaries receiving frontier boxes were not really on the frontier. The securing of missionaries for the Indian Territory had not escaped his attention. WMU was not supporting missions, it was directing them!

Annie was not going to take this sitting down. She couldn't believe this was the same Dr. Bell who had happily accepted WMU's help when he was head of the Sunday School Board. Not taking time to respond with a letter, Annie sent him a telegram, asking if he would print her reply to his editorial. To his credit, he agreed.

When her friends read Annie's reply, they were amazed. "It's so . . . mild," they noted. Wisely, Annie had not breathed fire into her words, but tried to strike a reasoning tone.

One bright spot in April was that on the 18th of the month Annie's cousin Mary Grace Levering Evans and her husband, Philip, were appointed as missionaries to China.

That spring Annie set off for a trip through Virginia, the Carolinas, and Georgia. She wanted to spur interest in the women missionaries for the Indian Territory. She spoke in as many places as possible, holding always to two rules: men must never invade the sanctity of a women's meeting, while as many women as possible must be reached.

In May, Annie, Mrs. John Barker of Virginia, and Mrs. J. D. Easterlin of Georgia visited the Home Mission Board to discuss some matters. Each woman waited her turn to be called into the meeting concerning her project. When Annie was called she told of the offer to support two missionaries, and asked for precise instructions about the box work. If there was a problem with the way WMU was handling it, she wanted to know.

The subject came up again at the Southern Baptist Convention in New Orleans that same month. The state Baptist papers painted the issue as one of dissatisfaction with WMU leadership, claiming the women wanted to run everything. This accusation bothered Annie to no end, but more was to come. In June, Dr. Bell printed an article by Annie in which she repeated comments of appreciation for WMU by Dr. Willingham, Dr. Kerfoot, and Dr. Frost at the Convention. Dr. Bell said he agreed with the comments, then undercut them by saying he claimed the right to criticize the organization because of his long friendship with WMU.

Georgia WMU showed their support of Annie and WMU policy by passing resolutions of support. Annie, along with some of her advisors and friends, guessed that Dr. Bell was in a roundabout way attacking Dr. Kerfoot through Annie. It was well known how loyal Annie was to him.

Baltimore, Late 1901

Sad news reached Annie in June, while she was busy defending herself and WMU from T. P. Bell and planning more travels. Dr. Kerfoot had died. Not only had Annie respected him as her pastor, she had been depending on him for direction in the New Century Movement. "He will be sorely missed," she said to herself and others.

Dr. F. C. McConnell succeeded Dr. Kerfoot as corresponding secretary of the Home Mission Board. In July, Annie received some measure of consolation for Dr. Bell's attacks. The Board praised WMU for its work with the boxes and approved the recommendations concerning that project. Also, two missionaries, Kate D. Perry of Texas and Kate Hanson of Washington, D.C., were appointed to the mining district of Indian Territory. Their support would be provided by Georgia WMU and Virginia WMU.

Also in July, Eutaw Place had a big farewell service for the Evanses, who were headed to Yang Chow, China. Junius W. Millard, now Annie's pastor, had received any number of helpful suggestions from her about the service. As it progressed, Annie fervently hoped and prayed it would stimulate more interest in foreign missions in her church. But also there drifted through her mind the thought of another service, so long ago now, when Jane had gone to China. Then there was the time she met and then said good-bye to Anne Luther Bagby in this same church. "So many dear people have come through this church as missionaries."

As always, Annie urged the women to pray harder for missionaries. The longer she was in WMU work, the more missionaries she met personally. She taught the societies to pray by the Golden Rule: pray for the missionaries as you would wish to be prayed for if *you* were the missionary.

In August and September, Annie made another marathon tour. She traveled 2,250 miles in 50 days and stopped in 30 places. She spent time in Virginia, Tennessee, Kentucky, and Maryland. The Tennessee women managed to catch Annie off guard.

"Miss Annie, we have a wonderful surprise for you," one of her Tennessee hostesses said. Another quilt? This was what people normally wanted to give her; she could have had hundreds if she accepted them.

It was not a quilt, nor homemade biscuits. The women had arranged for her to spend a week resting at Monteagle, a resort in the mountains. Annie was taken aback that they would make such a decision for her, but then discovered that the Stakely family would vacation there. An excellent opportunity to visit with Mrs. Stakely and get some work done, Annie saw. The two leaders did confer that week, but Annie rested, too.

Besides speaking to societies on her trip she met with WMU executive committees, talked with Dr. Frost, and addressed the National Baptist Women's meeting in September. She had been asked to speak on the why and how of women's organizations: why have them and how did they work?

Annie was gaining more and more respect for the black Baptist women. Nannie Helen Burroughs was a wonder, and the leadership quality of many of the women was first-rate. She felt her appearance at this September meeting was very important, and prepared herself thoroughly beforehand. While in Nashville in August she met with black women from societies in nine churches, and visited with Mrs. V. W. Broughton, the recording secretary of the Woman's Convention. She visited their publishing house, toured Fisk University and Roger Williams (two respected schools for blacks), and talked with black men missions leaders about ways to help the women. Through it all, Annie wanted to be a helper, not a boss.

Though Annie thoroughly enjoyed being with the National Baptist women, she was anxious about the possible criticism of Northern Baptists, who also worked with the black Baptists. And she still feared a man might come in, since Northern Baptists allowed mixed meetings. Annie would allow men to address WMU meetings, but they had to leave as soon as they stopped talking.

When the meeting was convened in Cincinnati, Anna Schimp was with Annie. Since Annie would be called to speak, she was given a seat of honor on the front row. It quickly became obvious some men had managed to infiltrate the meeting and wanted to stay.

"Please leave," the presiding officer asked the men over and over. Annie dared not turn around, but sat like a stone. From her vantage point, Anna Schimp amused herself watching one of the women kindly but firmly escort the men out of the gallery. Annie was safe.

Annie found anew that she was among friends at the National Baptist meeting. She helped with the organization when asked, pledged her cooperation and support, and encouraged the women.

"How did the meeting go?" someone asked Nannie Helen Burroughs later.

"Miss Armstrong is a trail blazer," said Miss Burroughs. "She delivered one of the most inspiring addresses of the entire Convention."

Most of Annie's co-workers and loved ones thought she had traveled enough in 1901, but she thought differently.

"I must not neglect Maryland WMU," Annie reminded herself and others. To that end, in her role as state leader, she went to the Eastern Shore in November. Faithful Anna Schimp went with her, taking care of the business details as usual so Annie would be free to speak and organize.

For hardship, Annie decided, the frontier in summer had nothing on the Eastern Shore in winter. In four days she met women in six churches, taking long train and buggy trips to reach her destination. At one stop she stumbled in exhausted at 3:00 A.M. Annie could stay up half the night writing or talking with women, but this was a bit much, even for her. One freezing night she stayed in a bedroom with four broken window panes and watched the ice form around her. Instead of feeling sorry for herself, it just made her more determined to help faithful Baptists who kept church alive under such conditions.

Baltimore, 1902

Annie was having a rough go of it with the Home Mission Board. First, it had declined her idea of establishing the Kerfoot Memorial Fund which would have increased the Church Building and Loan Fund. Then, the Board dragged its collective feet on paying half salary for two women to work among black women in southern states. She and R. H. Boyd, National Baptist Convention home missions leader, had discussed the matter. He would secure half the salary for a general missionary. Annie was certain she could find someone to pay half of Nannie Helen Burroughs's salary. The SBC Home Mission Board could pay the other half of each salary.

The Home Mission Board finally answered Annie, and in that answer she thought she could see the hand of T. P. Bell.

"So they do not have 'sufficient information,' eh?" Annie murmured to herself as she read the reply. The Board had also never received an application from the National Baptist Home Mission Board. When she read that, Annie hit the roof. She dashed off an angry letter to Dr. Tichenor, who was now secretary emeritus, complaining that no one had told her the National Baptists had to apply.

Finally, in March, the Home Mission Board approved appointment of two black field missionaries.

"And I could have been in Cuba while all this was going on," Annie thought wryly. Dr. McConnell had kindly invited her to join the Frosts and some others for a trip to Cuba in January. How she would have loved to have seen the beautiful island and the work she had supported for so long! But, between work and moving WMU headquarters to North Howard Street, it simply wasn't possible. Besides, she and Anna Schimp would be gone for three weeks starting in February.

Annie had never met the workers in Florida, and yearned to go there. Since she believed in making every minute count, she planned a few other stops along the 3,300-mile route: Louisiana, the Home Mission Board, the Stakely residence, and so forth.

It was a miserable experience. "Doesn't it ever stop raining?" the two women asked each other. Even balmy Florida was cold in the rain in February. As usual, the bad weather made Annie's neuralgia flare. Most women did not suspect, however, that their regal looking leader was in great pain for much of her visit.

She made a tremendous impression. Mrs. Chipley spoke for many of the women when she wrote, "She is a wonderful woman and a most delightful one, too. It was a great privilege and a great joy to be with her." She doubted anywhere was there a "wiser, nobler, more consecrated Christian" than Annie Armstrong.

"A telegram for you, Miss Annie." She was still in Florida when the dreaded piece of paper arrived. She was not expecting a message, so it was probably bad news. Annie ripped it open and was not disappointed. It was very bad news.

"What's wrong, Annie?" Anna asked sympathetically.

"I must go home!" Annie cried, and flew off to pack. The telegram was from Mamie; Alice was terribly ill with some type of fever. Annie rushed home, and the two sisters, one younger, one older, stood watch over Alice.

9
The Training School

Baltimore, 1902

With tender care from her sisters, Alice finally recovered, and Annie could give her full attention to promoting missions again. She began to plan her next big trip. Her itinerary would include the western strip of Oklahoma and the Indian Territory. On the way back she would stop in Missouri and Texas, and go into Mexico. Her total miles traveled this time would be 8,500; she would be gone 80 days.

"Why is Miss Annie going to the Indian Territory again so soon? She was only there two years ago." The WMU and church members who brought this up received a frank answer. Annie wasn't going to visit the missionaries again. She was going to secure that region for Southern Baptists and encourage frontier and Indian Christian women to lend their own support to missions work. It was time for them to be giving as well as receiving.

As for Mexico, Annie's main objective was to silence criticism that she cared more about home missionaries than their foreign counterparts. "I will make special efforts for Dr. T. P. Bell to know of my visit," Annie promised herself as she packed. He was still one of her harshest critics.

Annie boarded the train again for Indian Territory, with plenty of notebooks in case new and interesting things happened. It wasn't long before she began writing down her new adventures and experiences. She saw a Mormon hotel and a Mexican palace. Her heavy eastern clothes did not distress her as much as what she saw: mile after mile empty of any church or missionary; poverty beyond even her descriptive powers; entrenched superstition and violence. There were other experiences, however, that touched her to the quick and reaffirmed her faith that "blessed are ye who sow beside the waters."

On the sun-bleached Oklahoma plains a rider on horseback appeared on the distance. As he came closer, it was obvious that he had traveled a long way looking for Miss Annie W. Armstrong. Most eastern ladies would have been fearful of a rider asking for them by name in such a place, but Annie was not. She greeted the man, who was a few years older than herself, like a long-lost friend. As they talked and laughed, the curious began to pick up bits and pieces of the story.

After the Civil War, Mary Armstrong tried to help Confederate soldiers who were going home from Union prisons in the North. With Mary, help always included spiritual support as well as physical. She had taught her children by example in all things, including witnessing to soldiers, some of whom were still only in their teens. That's why this man, who was now a home missionary, had received a Bible with the name Annie W. Armstrong written inside it, along with a heartfelt message of salvation through faith in Jesus Christ. Their paths crossed in a manner of speaking when he became a home missionary and realized the lady who was now working so hard to support the frontier missionaries was the same teenaged girl who had given him a Bible so very long ago. When he found she was on the frontier he got on his horse and rode 30 miles to meet her in person.

The events of this trip weren't always so touching, but they were exciting. At one town she boarded a train whose passengers and crew were still shaken from a robbery four hours earlier. Annie made up for missing this bloodcurdling experience by being on board a train when it wrecked in Mexico.

Everything she saw and felt was fodder for her notebooks. When she finally returned home, she wrote article after article about her trip, hoping to inspire women to do more for missions at home and abroad. The meeting with the soldier turned missionary appeared in the November 1902 issue of *Foreign Mission Journal.*

In some of her more restful moments, when Annie could read a bit and visit with her Baptist friends, she caught up on all that happened while she was out West. One tidbit she learned was that Southern Baptist Theological Seminary had begun allowing prospective women missionaries to attend classes starting with the 1902–3 school year. They were not considered actual students; but, still, it was something the seminary had been working toward for some time.

Annie sat up and took notice of this development. She had thought the matter had been put to rest, but apparently things had happened of which she was not aware. "Not the training school issue again," she groaned inwardly. Certain people, with good intentions, had been agitating for a training school for prospective women missionaries for some time. In theory, Annie liked the idea, for she knew it was a problem when unequipped women arrived on the missions field. But, she saw many problems in such a school. And, there were already two perfectly fine Northern Baptist training schools, one in Philadelphia and one in Chicago. She couldn't understand why her friends would be shocked that she would recommend Northern Baptist training schools when she wouldn't recommend anything else Northern Baptist. They were good schools.

While 1902 was a wonderful year for her missions work, it was turning out to be dismal for Annie's personal finances. She had always resisted taking a salary when she was financially comfortable, echoing with David, "I will not give to the Lord that which cost me nothing." Now she was receiving less from her personal investments; but, as usual, tried to keep this private. She still did not want to take a salary when money got tight. How could she ask other women to give of themselves freely if she were not willing to do so?

"Besides," she argued, "If the corresponding secretary takes a salary, the state officers would expect payment, and it would be assumed that office expenses would decrease." Annie was a canny businesswoman. She knew that if she were paid, the price of stamps and printing and paper would stay the same, but their funds for such expenses might be cut, or given with the dreaded criticism that women didn't know how to manage.

Dr. Willingham, however, had learned a few things about working with Annie. He knew that she was stubborn, but that even she could be gotten around, sometimes. He talked things over with Dr. Frost and Dr. McConnell. The three men agreed: they wanted Annie to have enough money to live on decently. Certainly no one would expect a man to work for free as she had done all these years. It seemed really unjust, they told each other, that Miss Annie was not compensated for her work.

The Foreign Mission Board secretary stuck his neck out and wrote the WMU Executive Committee. "The Foreign Mission Board recommends that $750 a year be appropriated to the WMU corresponding secretary," he began, adding that the three boards would make equal appropriations. He also made it clear that they had not discussed the proposal with Annie. She had not been part of the idea at all.

Then he again began writing, this time to Annie. He enclosed a copy of the letter to the WMU Executive Committee. Now she couldn't just reject the suggestion out of hand. It was a recommendation from a Board; Annie was required to allow WMU to entertain the recommendation at Annual Meeting.

When Annie read the letter, her face fell. She did not want this! Why were men always trying to make her do things she didn't want to do? One had shown her picture at the orphanage Christmas party. Now one was trying to make her take a salary. Even Dr. Frost had not respected her desire to avoid speaking to men, when he sneaked into a meeting and lay down in a back pew so he could listen unseen. She could still remember the silly grin of satisfaction on his face when he sat up at the end of her speech. But Dr. Willingham had arranged things very well.

The WMU, SBC, vice-presidents received a letter from Annie in December about the salary. "It has been the joy of my life to give my services freely, and my hope never to be required to take one." It was such an odd situation, many of them remarked, to be trying to force someone to take money.

Annie wrote Mrs. Stakely that she would not attend the next year's Annual Meeting in Savannah. She couldn't preside over the vote since it affected her, and her very presence at the meeting might influence the women.

"This is just too, too embarrassing," Annie muttered.

Montgomery, February 1903

Annie and Mrs. Stakely were sitting together, planning the Annual Meeting. Annie kept insisting she did not want a salary, that she was quite nervous about the whole affair. If she needed money, she hedged, she could look for other ways to find it. Her president tactfully presented arguments for taking the salary. After all, this was not just about Annie; there would be other corresponding secretaries after her. Not all might be financially independent.

Mrs. Stakely's own family money troubles had made her sensitive to the needs of others.

As they talked, Annie's knowledge of what was going on in each state became clear. She had traveled so much and communicated so frequently with the state WMU leaders, she had almost an instinct for what each state needed. Those instincts did not always work when Annie dealt with her counterparts. Then the needs of WMU could blind her to what was going on around her. She had held a business meeting with Fannie Heck in Philadelphia when that young president was sick. Now, she didn't seem to notice what most women would have seen, although they might not have called attention to it.

Annie finally said good-bye to Mrs. Stakely. After she left, the president thought, "Does she not realize my condition?"

Baltimore, April 1903

Annie would not let the salary issue distract her from the training school anymore. She wrote the Board secretaries to suggest how to go about establishing such a school for women.

"I appreciate that you recognize the need for this, perhaps even more fully than I do, so it is not necessary for me to take your time or mine in advocating such a departure," she wrote.

She then went on to suggest that she would ask someone to present a resolution at Annual Meeting to appoint a committee to discuss the matter with the secretaries of the Home and Foreign Mission Boards. The committee would then bring a report in May 1904 as to whether it was advisable to have such a school "under the auspices of the Woman's Missionary Union." If it were deemed advisable, the committee should also be ready to suggest a location.

There was no endowment for such a school, so she suggested that students from Baptist colleges or women's schools support the school until such an endowment should be established.

The secretaries wanted a school, but shook their heads over the suggestion that students could themselves support a school. They urged Annie to go ahead with the resolution, with a few changes suggested by Dr. Willingham.

Baltimore and Montgomery, June 1903

A mere 16 days before Annual Meeting, a stunned Annie Armstrong read and reread the letter from Jessie Stakely. She wasn't going to be at Savannah because of her present condition. The 41-year-old mother of four was in the family way again, and her baby was due at the same time as Annual Meeting. "What do I do? What do I do?" Annie wondered. She could never just come right out and say that the WMU president was pregnant! That would be unforgivably vulgar. But she had just seen the woman in February. Surely an experienced mother would have known then when her baby was due to be born.

"She knew in February she wasn't going to be at the Annual Meeting, and didn't tell me," Annie said to herself.

Without thinking, Annie wrote Mrs. Stakely a note expressing her astonishment that she wasn't told during their visit. Then she sent a copy of Mrs. Stakely's letter to the WMU vice-presidents. If anyone was going to tell them Mrs. Stakely was in her present condition, surely it should be Mrs. Stakely, not Annie.

A few days later, Dr. Stakely found his wife visibly upset. She handed him Annie's note, and told him Annie had taken it upon herself to send copies of private correspondence to apparently half the world.

Dr. Stakely reacted as any man does when his pregnant wife is distressed. All his protective instincts came to the surface. He was livid. What was wrong with Miss Armstrong? She was just here in February. Couldn't she tell when another woman was nearly six months along? The thought did not cross his mind that as a childless woman, Annie might really not see the signs of pregnancy in someone else. Nor did he stop to think that his wife had led Annie to believe she would be at this meeting, where so much was emotionally invested.

He wrote his own note, short and terse, to several people. He called Annie's actions "offensive and humiliating." When Annie found out, she felt very wronged. Mrs. Stakely had not said that was a private correspondence. She was trying to do right by the woman by letting her speak for herself. Perhaps Dr. Willingham could help her feel her way through this mess. She certainly didn't want to offend anyone else . . . "but I must defend myself," Annie felt.

Dr. Willingham urged Annie not to show Mrs. Stakely's letter publicly, but show it to certain individual committee members. Then, given human nature, she could trust them to spread the word that the letter had not been labeled private. Annie gratefully followed his advice, and was gratified when the WMU Executive Committee went on record approving her actions and disapproving Dr. Stakely's letter.

Since Mrs. Stakely was not going to attend Annual Meeting, Annie had to find a presiding officer. The WMU rules called for the Maryland vice-president to take over. Mrs. John Eager was in frail health, but agreed to preside. "If it will help Miss Annie," she said sweetly.

Savannah, June 1903

Annie stood before the women and forced herself to read the letter from Dr. Willingham. She wanted to cringe from embarrassment, but she got through it. She also read her December response to the recommendation, and fled the meeting to take refuge in her hotel.

While there, she wondered what Cousin Joshua and his family were doing at that moment. He had invited her to go with them to visit the Evanses in China. He added to the temptation by saying, "And, we'll stop off in Japan and a few other countries—a sort of round the world trip, you know." She could have been with them now, in the middle of the Pacific Ocean in a storm, or seasick, or threatened by pirates. All those possibilities looked much more inviting than hiding in a hotel while people voted on her.

Soon, someone was sent to the hotel to get her. She was told, "Only South Carolina has opposed a salary for the corresponding secretary." Annie squelched the urge to say, "Praise the Lord for South Carolina." Instead, she went back to the meeting, where she was greeted with the women singing the doxology. She was touched—but she still wasn't taking a salary.

Annie was relieved when business turned to the training school resolution. Mrs. George W. Truett of Texas delivered a paper, "The Demand for Trained Women Workers." Immediately after, delegates adopted a resolution that the SBC should appoint a committee of seven, three of whom would be the Board secretaries. This committee would work with a WMU committee of seven to consider a training school. The SBC, in session at the same time, also adopted the WMU resolution.

Before the meeting was over, Annie saw Lillie Barker voted in as the new president. This was fine with her. And, the women were told that on the eve of the meeting Mrs. Stakely had given birth.

Before leaving Savannah, Annie asked Mrs. Eager to call an Executive Committee meeting in June. She had something to discuss with the members. In the meantime, she had more trips to plan. She had already made one springtime sweep through the South. It was a worthwhile trip, but how she missed Anna Schimp! It was much more fun traveling with the merry Swiss woman. She hoped Anna would go with her from now on.

Tennessee, August 1903

"We hate to see you leave us, Miss Annie." The woman looked up at Annie and was rewarded with a warm smile.

"It's time to go to the BYPUA meeting in Atlanta, I'm afraid." She continued packing and chatting with her hostess. She had traveled 3,000 miles to 5 states, but most of her time had been in beautiful Tennessee. Now, with the Baptist Young People's Union of America (BYPUA) meeting coming up, she had to say good-bye. She had many ideas for strengthening the work and inspiring Baptist young people to be missions-minded—doers, not talkers, was what she wanted.

With that in mind, she had obtained from the boards specific projects that the young people could help with: the Bible fund, schools in Mexico and other countries, church houses in Cuba, and mission Sunday Schools. She had already been working on ways to put missions information into the hands of the young people. Knowledge was power, she told herself again as she reached Atlanta.

Out West, Fall 1903

"Why do you have to go out West again?" Annie was getting used to being confronted with that question. To many people, travel out West for a woman her age was equated with torture.

"The Northern Baptist women missionaries travel and organize societies in Indian Territory. It is essential I attend the annual meeting in Indian Territory this year," she answered firmly. She still feared that Southern Baptists were going to lose the Indian Territory altogether if action weren't taken.

"I love the women of that place so much, I wish I could be their secretary. I'd give up the work here if it were possible," she said to Alice as she packed.

"So you've told me," patient Alice replied, and sighed, just a little.

Alice waved good-bye to Annie and waited for her to return from her 40-day sojourn covering 4,350 miles. She prayed for her protection and went back to her writing.

The WMU offices and the mission rooms seemed empty without Annie's presence filling them, but the work could continue.

"It's amazing how Miss Annie gets everything done in advance," one volunteer marveled. "She's got the literature orders filled, the new literature at the printer, all the correspondence up-to-date—everything runs so smoothly."

"They don't call her Strong Arm for nothing," another volunteer answered.

Baltimore, Late 1903

When Annie returned from her highly satisfactory visit out West, she hit the training school question head-on. She wished she had done more sooner. Back in 1895, the Texas women had wanted a training school. Then in 1900 a missionary named Simmons had approached what seemed to Annie to be most of the Southern Baptist Convention about starting such a school. Southern Seminary had taken the idea and run off with it like . . . Annie searched her mind for a comparison . . . like a western mustang taking the bit in its teeth. At least, that was the way it seemed to her. To other people, she was seen as an obstacle in the way of progress, she knew.

Well, there was progress now. She and Mrs. Barker and five other women made up the WMU Training School Committee. The Board secretaries were on the SBC committee, which was chaired by W. J. Northen, a Southern Seminary trustee. It had been agreed in Savannah that young women missionaries needed more training. The committee had formed three subcommittees, and Annie had been assigned as chair of the Curriculum Committee. Dr. Willingham, Dr. McConnell, and Mrs. Chipley (her friend from Florida) were on the committee. Looking around at the coed committee of Southern Baptist leadership, it seemed ages ago that Alice's presence on a church committee shocked Eutaw Place.

Now Annie had gathered prospectuses from different mission board who operated training schools, and had visited four personally. She also asked for information from Southern Seminary. She bundled up copies of her research and sent them to her committee members for study.

Baltimore, Winter 1904

Annie sent out her New Year's cards to friends. Emblazoned on it was the message, "We are laborers together with God." She needed the reminder, for winter of 1904 was not starting out well. The weather was horrible, with ice and snow making the streets positively dangerous. Finally, in early February, there was a thaw that left the streets a slushy swamp. At least the weather was milder, and there was a breeze blowing.

Disaster struck the next morning, a Sunday. Fire broke out in a downtown dry goods store. It raged for 30 hours and devoured everything in its path, which was most of the Baltimore business and financial district. In 70 city blocks, 2,000 buildings had burned to the ground. The fire would cost Baltimore millions of dollars.

Annie was torn by her fears for her family, for the rest of Baltimore, and for the mission rooms. Since the phone service was down, she went in search of news and found plenty.

"The governor has declared tomorrow a legal holiday," she was told. "That way the remaining banks can close and there won't be a run on them. You know how people panic. The wharves are charred to a crisp, the newspaper offices are gone, people have lost everything."

When she saw Eugene on Monday morning, he looked pale and grim. "I do not know that I have a dollar left," he said. His bank had burned to the ground, and so had his coffee import company. Commerce Street, where the family conducted much business, was practically gone. Annie and Alice were not unscathed. They owned three warehouses and a portion of two more. All were ashes. Since the prevailing belief was that businesses usually weren't a total loss in case of fire, the family had not carried as much insurance as needed to replace the buildings.

Annie wrote to Dr. Willingham of what she called "the fearful calamity." Though she had great faith, Annie was not naive. She knew it was devastating. Her heart ached for those who lost their life savings. It was pitiful when people approached her saying, "Miss Annie, could we rent a room from you? We have nowhere to go." She wished she could take in all the homeless, but she and Alice were already sharing the row house with a minister and his wife. There was no more room. She tossed and turned at night thinking about what to do.

She marched down to the mission rooms and found them safe. The post office was safe too, so that the mail was only delayed an hour. The volunteers and clerks showed up for work. It was almost eerie for such disaster to be right outside their doors, and inside to hear the clack of typewriters and the rustle of literature being packed as if all was normal. Annie soon learned that it was far from normal for the mission rooms.

"Printers, box makers, the express, even cash for postage—it can't be gotten for love or money, Miss Annie," she was told.

"What of the week of prayer materials for next month?" She wondered. They had already been printed.

"Gone," they told her. "Gone up in flames with the printer's business." Along with the week of prayer literature was a leaflet written by Lansing Burrows which would have promoted the I. T. Tichenor Memorial Fund, a church building fund. How Annie hated knowing it too was gone!

She dashed off letters to states notifying them of the fire and urging them to go forward with the week of prayer observance, even without literature. She wrote articles for the state Baptist papers about what happened. She pressed on through what seemed like a bad dream. Once she asked for a ball of twine and found that even it couldn't be bought—there was none left.

She kept Dr. Willingham informed of everything. One letter revealed Annie's determination in the face of the disaster.

"The future, humanly speaking, is dark, but 'Man's extremity is God's opportunity.' For the present it is undoubtedly my duty to keep right on with WMU work. This I shall do, and use every power I possess in helping to advance same and carry out the plans which we have inaugurated. I would be recreant to the trust which I have assumed, or rather which I believe God has imposed on me, to do anything else until the annual meeting of the Woman's Missionary Union in Nashville."

Annie had already had several illnesses that winter; the stress of the cold weather and the fire made it worse. A health crisis could not be far away, her loved ones feared, and they were right.

One Saturday, Annie suddenly became lightheaded. Her legs felt like they had turned to water. She tried to catch herself as the room started to swim before her eyes. The next thing she knew, she was confined to bed for a day of complete rest, though it would take more than one day for her to fully recover.

While she was resting, there was a timid knock at the door. She called for the person to come in. Her visitor stepped inside carrying a food tray. A tantalizing aroma wafted around the bedroom.

"I brought your dinner to you, Miss Annie." It was the wife of the minister who was boarding with them. A meal brought to her room—this was a novelty! Annie was touched and a little amused at the way the minister's family tried to show their concern for her by constant visits and other little attentions. While this was going on, Annie tried numerous remedies, including a visit to the dentist, to see if it would help her recover.

Finally, the literature was printed, though Annie was not really sure how it happened. She attributed the results to God and kept on working. Now feeling better, she continued her church work, the mothers' meetings at Eutaw Place, and her other interests in addition to WMU responsibilities. Though WMU did not have societies just for young women, Annie reached out to them with college visits.

Annie deeply wanted to see the I. T. Tichenor Memorial Fund succeed, and sent out 1,000 letters to individuals. She promoted the Yang Chow Hospital where her Evans relatives worked. But in the back of her mind, while all this wonderful work was progressing, the training school problem still simmered.

The problem began to heat up when yet another article advocating a training school appeared in an April issue of the *Baptist Argus*. In it Dr. Mullins said that earlier, seminary trustees had voted to establish a training school in connection with the seminary. Annie had already fended off two attempts by the seminary to get WMU, SBC, to accept its classrooms for training school use. Now he made strong arguments for why Louisville was the right place to locate the school. Annie could read between the lines as well as anybody. This was the same as saying, "We already have a training school, and this seminary is the right place for it."

Annie, however, was more and more convinced the seminary was the wrong place for it. She did not want young women missionaries sitting in classes where they could be inflamed with talk about preaching. Furthermore, she did not want the professors and male students to see the training school as a marriage bureau. There were already jokes about that, and some serious comments, and she felt it insulting to WMU and to the young women themselves.

As if things weren't complicated enough, Maryland Baptist state secretary Elridge B. Hatcher wanted a training school in Baltimore. The Woman's State Mission Society and the Ministers' Conference both endorsed the idea. Annie kept her distance.

"As a member of the joint Southern Baptist Convention–Woman's Missionary Union committee on a training school, I have no opinion on the Baltimore school," was all she would say.

Atlanta, Spring 1904

Annie had come to Atlanta to visit Baron DeKalb Gray, the new corresponding secretary for the Home Mission Board. He had just taken the position the year before, and she was still trying to form a good working relationship with him. While she was in Atlanta, she visited several colleges and churches, then made a brief stop in Greenville, South Carolina, on the way home.

"Train travel is so much better now that they have sleepers," Annie told herself as she settled back for a night's rest on the train. She was now a seasoned traveler and could sleep under noisy conditions that would have kept her awake when she made her first trip to the Indian Territory. Annie went to sleep praying for the rest of the trip. She was going to New York to see a possible donor for WMU, SBC, and would stop in Philadelphia and Washington, too. In New York she wanted to see Ellis Island. With Marie Buhlmaier she had witnessed the immigrants landing in Baltimore, but that would be nothing compared to Ellis Island, she knew. And in Philadelphia and Washington there would be training schools to tour.

Nashville, May 1904

It was the Southern Baptist Convention and committee chair W. J. Northen was reporting for the joint training school committee. Annie had found a way to use the article by President Mullins to put a stop to the training school, she was certain. She had offered resolutions which the committee accepted.

"Since Southern Seminary had not given notice before 1903 that there was already a Training School for Women Missionaries in connection with the seminary at Louisville, and since President Mullins had publicly announced this school in the April 7, 1904, issue of the *Baptist Argus*, the committee recommended taking no action and leaving the subject with the seminary." This caused a great deal of dismay among training school advocates. This was not what they had meant to happen!

Then, when Annie thought the situation was solved, Dr. Frost offered a new resolution. She stared as he brought a resolution that the SBC commend the work Southern Seminary was doing and encourage the seminary to enlarge and better equip the work of the Training School Department.

She could simply not believe what she was hearing. How could he do this to her? He had just ignored the wishes of the rest of the committee and given the SBC a way to go ahead with the school. Annie would never, ever feel the same way about Dr. Frost again.

Barely was the meeting over before the Kentucky women began supporting the training school. Eliza Broadus had been opposed to the school while her powerful father, John A. Broadus, had been living. After he died and she was no longer under his influence, Eliza suddenly had a conversion experience where the school was concerned. A local committee of Louisville women was appointed and began securing a home and furnishings for the women students. Kentucky WMU secured the support of women in several other states.

Annie was busy trying to think of a way out or around this. She knew that she had to be very careful about WMU support for any type of school. If WMU were to do anything for any theological school at home or abroad, she would be accused of being unfair to Southern Seminary. But while she was busy with the training school question, she continued her other work. WMU couldn't come to a standstill because of one dilemma.

Out West Again, August–September 1904

Annie was still fearful the SBC would lose Oklahoma and the Indian Territory. To lend her support, she planned to attend the conventions in those two areas, but she wasn't going alone. After a brief stop in St. Louis to see the Exposition and admire the Baptist exhibit run by the Missouri Baptist women, Annie went to Clinton, Missouri, to meet her traveling companion. She had invited a newly appointed home missionary and graduate of the Philadelphia training school to travel with her. She could help orient the young woman to the work until they reached Oklahoma. Annie felt a special interest in this young woman: South Carolina women were supporting her.

One look at Lura Stump told Annie the young missionary was terrified. Lura was experienced in city missions work, but trembled at the thought of the frontier and Indians. Annie spent two-and-a-half days with her in the Delaware Indian Association and visited the Kiowas. During that time, Annie saw clear evidence that God was guiding the missions work. She wrote to South Carolina, "See the steps: the young women of South Carolina decide to support a missionary to the Osage Indians. A timid young girl starts to go to them. A minister on the field has already decided to go to these same Indians. A delegation of 28 Kiowas visits them just at this time to recommend Christianity. A Christian interpreter is ready to do the needed work, and the needed money to support him is supplied. Can we doubt that God's Hand is guiding this infant mission and that He will abundantly bless the work?"

Jacksonville, Florida, January 1905

Annie had returned to Florida for the WMU Annual Meeting there. To her pleasure, she had been asked to speak at the children's meeting. Her topic was "Squaws and Papooses." She told the children colorful, touching stories about frontier missions, missionaries, and Indian Christians.

Annie spent a total of two weeks in Florida. ("And no horrible telegram from home this time," she told herself.) She spent one week in South Carolina, and then stopped off in North Carolina and Virginia on the way home.

Mountain Country, March 1905

Albert E. Brown had kindly offered to conduct a tour of mountain schools for Annie. The only drawback was that if she wanted to see schools in session, she had to go when the weather was bad. March in the mountains of North Carolina, Kentucky, and Tennessee could be rainy and cold. Combined with the poor roads, it made for tough going. Annie found herself riding in carriages and buggies for part of her 2,125-mile trip.

It was worth it, though. Annie loved the mountain schools—the beautiful scenery, the dedicated teachers, the children who struggled against such poverty and hardship. She visited 16 places and made 27 talks in 19 days. Then she went home and wrote a support leaflet called "Lengthen Cords and Strengthen Stakes" so that all Southern Baptists would know about the needs of the mountain schools. Annie never went anywhere just to be a tourist; it was always for the sake of encouragement and information.

Writing the leaflet was so much more fun than writing letters to Dr. Frost to complain about his associate, I. J. Van Ness. He was the editorial secretary at the Sunday

School Board, and he had been unforgivably rude, in Annie's opinion.

It had all started when—last month? He had ignored her request for material for Marie. The Board had always provided her literature and Gospels for her work with the immigrants. Because Annie had heard Dr. Frost was ill, she had wanted to avoid bothering him and had written Mr. Van Ness. He had ignored her! This was even more irritating because Annie wrote reams of material for the Sunday School quarterlies, without pay and often without a byline. She had worked for Mr. Van Ness. Yet, this was not the first time he had ignored a letter from her.

Forgetting that Dr. Frost was sick, she wrote him. "I would think that Dr. Van Ness' silence was due to my letter going astray, but I have learned through experience that Dr. Van Ness does not think it necessary to reply to letters and only writes when he desires some material sent to him for his editorial work." She thought for a moment, then added that she would have to tell the Home Mission Board the missionaries did not have Gospels and would have to look elsewhere for literature. She also reminded Dr. Frost of all that she had written for Dr. Van Ness. She had tried to be the friend of the Sunday School Board and support it in every way, and did not understand being treated this way. Before she had just been unappreciated; now she was being slighted completely.

Then she turned her sights on Dr. Van Ness. In the letter to him she assured him he need not worry about bothering with manuscripts from her again. She could use her time in better ways. Also, she would never again ask the Board to send materials to missionaries or anyone else. When Annie was finished with someone, she was finished all the way.

She finally got a reply to her letters, this time from Dr. Frost. He was not playing peacemaker as he had done with Lansing Burrows and Fannie Heck. His letter sounded as if he were asking Annie to apologize. She refused, since it "is perfectly immaterial to you and Dr. Van Ness what the Corresponding Secretary of the Woman's Missionary Union may think. I know it is your desire and Dr. Van Ness' to please our Heavenly Father, and if that has been done it makes no difference what anyone else thinks."

Her comment about ignoring what she thought was about much more than literature, and Dr. Frost knew it. She had never stopped bringing up his resolution at the SBC last May. He could not leave well enough alone, and now there was all this trouble because of it. Annie felt ill used for all her work for the Board and for Dr. Frost personally.

Baltimore, April 1905

The training school advocates had made their next move. Mrs. Barker, the WMU president, had received a letter signed by five WMU, SBC, vice-presidents, including Eliza Broadus, asking her to place the training school on the agenda for the 1905 Annual Meeting. Mrs. Barker refused, on the grounds that the whole matter had been referred to the seminary by the SBC. She did allow, however, that the matter could be brought to the floor by resolution.

The letters and articles about the training school were flying at this point. The only one not receiving letters, it seemed to Annie, was the corresponding secretary of WMU. Mrs. George B. Eager, the chair of the Louisville committee, had written an article for the *Christian Index*, supporting the training school and the home for young women. T. P. Bell, of course, advocated support for the home. This article was later enclosed in a letter from the Louisville committee to the WMU, SBC, vice-presidents, asking for their support.

"This is ridiculous," Annie growled to herself. "Pretending that the home for the women students and the training school are separate." If there were no training school, there would be no need for a women's residence. It was like trying to say a college was separate from its dormitories.

At least, Annie was gratified to learn, B. D. Gray had refused a request from the Louisville committee to recommend the training school to WMU. He knew full well what the resolutions had been at the SBC. It had been referred to the seminary, and it was not any of the Home Mission Board's business, as far as he was concerned.

No one on the training school side wrote to Annie. Her feelings were known, and after the way she had used Dr. Mullins's *Argus* article, who knew what she might do with a careless phrase in a letter?

Mrs. Barker and Alice were on Annie's side, but she wasn't sure who else was. Ultimately it did not matter. She knew what she believed, and would stand her ground. She had done so with Fannie Heck, with Northern Baptists, and with many others. But she had much thinking to do, because this time the cost of standing her ground might be very high. She would have to make up her mind if the price was too high to pay.

10
Changing Course

April 1905

She had had quite enough, Annie decided. The attempts to go behind her back and gain endorsement for the training school, coupled with the increasing attacks by T. P. Bell, had helped her make up her mind. As much as Annie loved missions and felt she was doing God's work, she was only human. She had self-respect and pride. But she *was* the corresponding secretary of WMU, and she would not continue to hold that title if she was to be treated with such disdain and disrespect.

Annie did what came naturally to her—put her feelings in a letter. She appealed to Dr. Willingham and tried to make him see her side of the issue. How would he feel, she wrote, if someone were trying to involve the Foreign Mission Board in a certain project and he were kept in the dark about it? Then she told him how matters stood.

"It savors very much of political wire pulling and I would say to you without the shadow of a doubt if the Woman's Missionary Union is prepared to endorse such actions they will at the Annual Meeting in Kansas have to select another Corresponding Secretary."

Dr. Willingham wrote back, trying to soothe Annie's feelings with his assurances that she should have been consulted on the matter. His kind words did not change

Annie's mind about quitting. And, if WMU acted over her objections, the organization would not only lose Annie's services, but those of Alice. The matter would come to a head in Kansas City. Annie was determined, but she was not looking forward to the confrontation that was certainly to come.

Kansas City, May 1905

Southern Seminary trustees milled around together in their meeting on May 11. The training school was the topic of the moment. Yes, they decided, leave the training school in Louisville.

"But," asked one trustee, "can we operate such an endeavor without the support of Woman's Missionary Union?" The consensus of his fellow trustees was a definite no. The trustees needed and wanted WMU support for the Woman's Missionary Training School. Dr. W. W. Landrum, the chair of the trustees' training school committee, drew the happy duty of expressing the trustees' wishes to the WMU Annual Meeting, where he knew the formidable Annie Armstrong was ready to oppose their desire. At least he didn't have to speak for the training school in the WMU meeting session. That would be the job of E. Y. Mullins.

Feelings ran high at the first session, which Mullins attended. The topic was broached when Miss M. Gibson, the president of the Scarrett Bible and Training School in Kansas City, spoke briefly. She invited the WMU women to visit the school. Then the real strategy began unfolding. Mrs. J. L. Burnham of Missouri offered a resolution that WMU, SBC, "endorse the Home for the young women attending the Woman's Missionary Training School in Louisville, and heartily commend the Home to the sympathy and help of State Central Committees."

Immediately, Annie moved to table the motion until that afternoon. She also asked to speak to the resolution. A voice rang out in reply.

"I ask that Dr. Mullins also have the privilege of speaking to the motion." Heads turned and the women saw that Mrs. S. E. Woody of Kentucky had made that request.

Graciously, Annie offered to give up the time of her opening address to Mullins so that he could speak first on the issue. She would speak later. This gracious act also ensured that she had time to think about what the seminary president said before she responded.

The women grew edgier as the day wore on. In the afternoon session Mullins spoke about the status of the school. He urged WMU, SBC, to offer financial support to the home of the female students. With that done, he made his exit. Now was the time for Annie to take her stand.

She read facts that she had gleaned from her detailed study of training schools. Then she offered her resignation. Women looked at each other. Had they heard correctly? Some wondered, but others knew they had heard aright. This woman's determination—and some felt, her stubbornness—was leading her to risk her entire career. She told the women forthrightly that she disapproved of the way the Louisville women had gone about promoting the training school, and she felt betrayed.

If Annie's words were a shock, Mrs. Barker's words were electrifying. After reading aloud letters concerning the proposal, she stated that she could no longer continue as WMU's national president. Annie had made her feelings only too plain, but many delegates had not known Mrs. Barker felt so strongly.

Even in the face of the threatened resignations, some delegates defended Louisville women. The vote was taken: Mrs. Burnham's resolution lost, but by a narrow margin of 25 to 22.

The fight was not over, however. It just changed course a little. While the Louisville women had led the charge in gathering support from denominational leaders, Annie noticed it was the Missouri women who brought the resolutions during the Annual Meeting. Had someone decided ahead of time that it really would look too much like the Louisville women were forcing the training school on WMU if they brought the resolutions? There was no way to know, but Annie listened as Mrs. W. F. Elliott of Missouri offered two resolutions. She called for prayerful consideration of the work being done by Southern Seminary and the desirability of providing a home for women students. She asked that the decision be made at a WMU Annual Meeting whether WMU would accept the responsibility of supporting that home. And, she wished the Louisville women to be commended for what they had done.

Annie waited as the vote was taken. She had let the women know that as far as she was concerned, the actions of the Louisville women were disloyal to her. She would know where she stood if the resolutions passed.

The wait was over. Mrs. Elliott was victorious, though Annie and her supporters knew the Missouri woman was simply expressing the feelings and wishes of many in the crowd—apparently the majority.

Later, the nominating committee brought its report. Annie and Mrs. Barker were reelected as corresponding secretary and president, respectively.

Annie and Mrs. Barker agreed to serve one more year, so that WMU's work would not be interrupted. During that year their replacements could be found. Annie promised to do everything she could to make it the best year WMU had ever had. Then she issued one more statement to the delegates. The tall woman looked majestic as she stood in front of the crowd in her long sweeping skirt and high-necked blouse.

In a clear voice Annie said, "In the coming year please do not write to ask me why I have made this decision. If you write, know that *I will not answer.*" There was no doubt she meant it, just as there was no doubt Alice meant it when she resigned her editorial position. As always, she stood beside her sister, figuratively as well as literally.

Annie left Kansas City exhausted, hurt, and angry. "I could sue a number of people for libel over this matter," she growled.

"Such as?" asked her friends.

"Mr. T. P. Bell for one, Eliza Broadus, several of the Southern Seminary professors and . . ." Annie paused as she went through her mental list of people who had wronged her, "the wife of the seminary financial agent!"

"Annie, why would you want to take people to court over this?" Though Christians were not immune to the temptation to sue each other, it was a horrible thought.

"Perhaps," she answered in a more controlled voice, "perhaps if the truth were known, no one else could be mistreated the way I have been." And the harsh treatment continued, although the WMU, SBC, Executive Committee supported her by letting it be known that they, too, would refuse renomination in 1906. Their action did nothing to protect her from the state Baptist newspapers.

"Under pressure of one of the Union's leaders—its veritable leader—the ladies first declined," said the *Biblical Recorder* of the training school resolution. "But on second thought they voted to give the department their support. This brought about quite an upstir, and the leader referred to gave her notice of her resignation." The paper did not let the issue go with merely reporting what happened. It pointed out that it was the custom of the English for a leader to resign when people refused to follow that leader in an important decision. Also, the paper stated that Baptist leaders were to do the will of the majority rather than try to push their own desires upon the followers.

Annie's friends and supporters had to endure the suggestion of the editor of the *Baptist Argus* that he knew several people who could take Annie's place. She, however, did not have to endure the request that followed. One day while going through the mail she opened a letter from the newspaper's business manager asking that she send the editor a complete list of state WMU secretaries. A stamped return envelope fluttered out. Annie threw the envelope into the wastebasket.

As each newspaper came out, it seemed there was fresh support for the training school, which Annie took as criticism of her. She saw that the *Religious Herald* urged Virginia women to cooperate with the Louisville women in providing for the training school students. She was not surprised that T. P. Bell was endorsing an appeal for the home from Mrs. S. E. Woody of Louisville.

Then a very different letter appeared in the *Maryland Baptist*. The unsigned letter urged the newspaper to print a complete discussion of having a training school attached to Southern Seminary, with arguments both for and against. The writer warned against having the school established in the same place "in which hundreds of young men ready to marry are being educated at the same time."

"Do you think Annie Armstrong wrote the letter?" one WMU member asked.

"Most likely," her friend answered.

"No!" snapped another woman. "When Annie Armstrong expresses an opinion, she has the courage to put her name to it." The women finally decided they would never know, but that as forthright as Annie had been about the training school, she would almost certainly have signed her name to any letter she wrote on the subject.

June 1905

Dr. Willingham opened a letter that he knew was from Annie Armstrong. The woman was such a prolific correspondent, he had learned to spot her letters in an instant. As he read the letter, the Board secretary could almost feel Annie's hurt as she tried to transfer it to the written page.

With amazement he noted that she was not only leaving WMU, SBC, but would not even support WMU in her church.

"You have full permission to assure those who desire changes that it is not only my unalterable determination (unless God should work a miracle) to sever my connections with the Woman's Missionary Union in May, but also to resign the presidency of the Woman's Baptist Home Mission Society of Maryland which I have held for nearly 24 years, and that of the Society of Eutaw Place Church which office I have also held for years. After the meeting of the convention in May 1906, I do not propose in any way, shape or form to have anything whatever to do in mission work as conducted by Southern Baptists, so even in Maryland none need fear my opposition to whatever plans they may desire to present."

As usual, Dr. Willingham had no magic words to soothe Annie's hurt feelings. He wrote back what he could: she was greatly esteemed. He knew of no attempt to boycott her. Ignore the state papers. Go on with the work.

Annie read Dr. Willingham's letter, looking for advice, encouragement, and, yes, sympathy. She pondered his words. He said go on with the work. He was a good friend, a wise man, and her brother in Christ. To go on with the Lord's work was good advice, indeed, and suited her own active nature. To Dr. Willingham's advice Annie added the reminder of her promises at Kansas City. While promising to try and make her last year in WMU the best, she had also said she would try to provide information to the state committees. She would visit the states during the summer and encourage the work there.

Annie painstakingly planned visits to Tennessee and Georgia to promote the hospital in Yang Chow and the Tichenor Memorial. As she wrote out ideas it occurred to her that she would need some type of literature to help the promotion. In short order she wrote a leaflet called "A Hospital for Yang Chow."

While all this was going on, Alice continued keeping house for herself and Annie. Alice had always known Annie detested housekeeping. It was Annie who needed to meet with the WMU central committees before she left office. It was Annie who had to travel on uncomfortable trains at all hours of the day and night. At least, she, Alice, could help pack and direct household affairs and manage the servants. If she worried about Annie overworking herself, she did not share her fears, although Annie's 31-day itinerary was enough to exhaust anyone.

After Annie returned home from the trip, she stayed in Baltimore only a few days and was on her way again. The long dresses and conservative hats and gloves were cleaned, pressed, and packed so Annie could visit the Indian Territory in September.

"Is this trip really necessary?" questioned a concerned church member at Eutaw Place.

"Annie is afraid that a new corresponding secretary will not understand the Indian Territory and the need to hold it for Southern Baptists," Alice explained.

"But so much travel! How can your sister hold out?" the woman asked.

"Annie says, 'Rewards await us yonder, work awaits us here,'" quoted Alice. "Besides, this trip will only last 12 days." Alice decided it was the better part of wisdom not to tell the concerned friends that the 12-day trip for Annie included 5 nights sleeping on the train, 18 meetings, 10 speaking engagements, and over 3,200 miles traveled.

She could also have told their friends that the traveling, as much as Annie disliked it, was painless compared to the barrage of attacks from Dr. T. P. Bell. It was hard for Alice to see her beloved sister so constantly criticized. Annie was leaving. She had promised to have absolutely nothing to do with Southern Baptist missions work ever again. What more did they want? Alice wondered.

No one seemed to know. In July, Bell had written another editorial about WMU and, without directly naming her, Annie.

"For several years past, there has been a growing dissatisfaction in various parts of the South over some of the ways which have been adopted by the leaders of the Woman's Missionary Union. It has been felt that there was too much of a one-person power in the organization—a power that was wielded with too little consideration for the views, and even the feelings of other interested workers. At Kansas City, the matter culminated, with the result that the leader of the Union announced her determination to resign her position."

Bell went on to make several other comments about how unfairly he had been criticized by WMU members and how he had offered his best talents to the organization. Annie was livid when she read the editorial. *He* had been criticized unjustly? *He* had given his best work to WMU? Outrageous! To whom could she turn to express her feelings?

The secretary of the Foreign Mission Board was hardly surprised when he opened the letter from Annie and read, "No words can express how indignant and hurt I feel." Dr. Willingham took in the gist of the rest of the letter. Annie felt T. P. Bell owed her a great debt and was ungrateful. She called the editorial abominable. Dr. Willingham sighed.

October 4, 1905

Annie sat down to compose her thoughts. She looked at the blank paper in front of her. This was going to be a difficult letter to write, but she must write it. She could not keep all these thoughts and feelings bottled up inside any longer. She was going to tell Frost exactly what she thought of his treatment of her. She still had to work with him in settling details such as the Mission Literature Department, but he would know exactly where they stood.

She accused him of being the one to let the training school advocates accuse her of opposing the Southern Baptist Convention because she did not think women should train to be preachers. He had acted inappropriately in making a resolution that was contrary to the spirit of the training school committee's report when he was a member of that very same committee!

"You did exactly wrong, and your action has caused already a great deal of trouble and will, I fear, result in much harm to the work." She had tried to help Frost so much in the past. Couldn't he have let someone else speak about what the Southern faculty wanted?

She echoed her fear that if women were in the same classes as men, they would want to become preachers. She told him she didn't expect him to answer her letter. And, she let him know that she knew he had suggested the name of Martha McIntosh Bell to take her place. She knew Bell would have support from Southern Seminary. In Kansas City, Annie had felt the full force of what happened when the seminary faculty and the Louisville women got behind an issue, so she predicted the same would happen if Bell were nominated.

She then ended the epistle by writing, "To sum up this whole matter I am standing for two principles; first, the unscripturalness of training women to be preachers, and second, for right methods in Southern Baptist mission work." Annie enclosed her nine-page history of the training school movement and asked him to read it.

When the letter arrived, Frost wasted no time in sending off an indignant reply that he had the right to judge for himself what God would have him do. Annie returned fire. Did she not have that right also? Yet instead she received persecution for following what she felt was God's leading.

"What I call in question is not persons differing from me in regard to the establishing of the so called Training School at Louisville, but the methods adopted by those who are advocating same."

And when it came to methods, she did not care for Frost's. He had caused her to suffer with letters, actions at the Southern Baptist Convention, and newspaper articles.

"You may say that you have nothing to do with some of these. My brother, this is true in a certain sense, but you are largely responsible for starting the ball rolling."

At least, Annie thought while in the middle of this letter battle, she had the support of the Woman's Baptist Home Mission Society of Maryland. She met with the Executive Committee October 5 and reported about the training school and T. P. Bell's unending attacks in the *Christian Index*. She also let them know she would relinquish leadership in the society as well as her office in WMU, SBC.

The committee's response could not have been more satisfying. The committee made plans to bring a resolution at the November annual meeting that the society could not endorse the training school and would instruct its delegates at the WMU Annual Meeting in May to vote against supporting the training school.

Baltimore, November 1905

The November winds blew hard and bitter cold around the row house on McCulloh Street. From the windows Annie could watch the dying leaves swirl to the ground and cover the frost-seared grass. Summer, when everything was green and promising, had ended too soon. She nursed her neuralgia as best she could and turned to writing letters, some of the hardest letters she would ever write, though she had expressed the same sentiments since the Kansas City meeting.

"I want no resting time in the sense of idleness, and so I shall as soon as I leave this work, turn my attention to other lines of Christian activity. I regret extremely that I cannot give what ability I have to the advancement of the work as done by Southern Baptists . . . but I now recognize that this will cause friction. . . . Many avenues are opening out before me. I am trying to listen for God's voice before making final decisions."

To Dr. Willingham she wrote, "I believe I should be perfectly miserable at the prospect of giving up this work in May, if I did not feel that God would give me something else to do for Him in other directions. It will have to be in our own church and along undenominational lines, but a number of openings in that direction are already presenting themselves to me."

Baltimore, February 1906

The articles and speeches about the training school continued to flow, and the attacks against Annie grew more hurtful and insulting. T. P. Bell decided to ridicule the charge that the training school would become a marriage bureau, and he managed to do it in such a way as to ridicule Annie as well.

"It might well have arisen in the fertile imagination of some maiden lady of uncertain age, who has come to look upon marriage as a dreadful thing, and especially a marriage between two Christians whose hearts are one in service of the master," he speculated.

Annie stayed silent, at least in her letters, about this attack. Alice and a few family members were the only ones who knew that Annie could have been a wife and mother serving the Lord in north China if she had accepted the marriage proposal made so many years ago. Of the few people who knew there had been a proposal, most were not sure which missionary, Hartwell or Rosewell Graves or perhaps someone else, had pursued Annie. Too, she had seen the beauty of the marriage between Mamie and her husband. She had been a friend and mentor to many frontier missionary couples. Annie was not against marriage, she had simply sacrificed a human commitment because of her commitment to God. But she would not dignify T. P. Bell's attack by explaining this.

Baltimore, Spring 1906

Annie and her Executive Committee sat together, comparing notes and voicing their ire. The Board secretaries had visited Baltimore to discuss the future of WMU, SBC. But instead of meeting with Annie and the Executive Committee, they had met with leading pastors and laymen! Did the secretaries honestly think that the leadership of WMU would allow its future to be decided by those outside the organization? Were the secretaries plotting something?

The women somehow managed to convey their annoyance and suspicions to the secretaries. Gray got wind of it and wrote Frost, wanting him to know the silly fears that Annie and Mrs. Charles Ammen, the chair of the nominating committee, had about the visit.

"It seems that she is entertaining the idea that we went to Baltimore to force headquarters on that city. I learned from another source that Miss Armstrong was filled with dread lest that was the ominous meaning of our visit." He wrote awhile longer, then came back to Annie.

"Miss Armstrong seems to be in great dread lest we would force Baltimore to have the headquarters there, when she has said publicly and in print that they could not be continued there."

Annie had said the headquarters could not continue in Baltimore. But, it did continue.

Chattanooga, May 1906

Annie boarded the train that would take her to her last WMU Annual Meeting. She was just a few weeks shy of her 56th birthday, and her life would be starting all over again, she thought. But first, she must put this last meeting behind her and give up her leadership. Perhaps then the criticism would stop. She was turning her back on the work that had been her life for 18 years. Surely that was a high enough price to pay to silence her critics.

The women, including Annie, spent most of an afternoon discussing the training school. The feelings of the Southern Seminary trustees were made known—they approved of the action. So did the WMU delegates. A resolution was brought to establish a training school. To the thrill of its supporters, the resolution passed by a wide margin. But one last snag appeared, as Mrs. Barker, in her last meeting as national president, ruled that according to WMU's constitution, for a new work to be taken up by WMU without previous notice, it must have a unanimous vote. The training school would be delayed at least for another year.

Annie tried to conduct herself at the last meeting with dignity and generosity. She used her final report to summarize her 18 years of work. On the Friday of the meeting, she told the women that the curios, many which had been personal gifts to her, were now her gifts to the Union. As she made a few other remarks, Annie saw that many women were wiping tears from their eyes. There was a closing prayer. Then she left to board the train back to Baltimore. That was how she wanted it.

After Annie left the room, Mrs. A. J. Wheeler of Tennessee spoke. "May we have a moment of silent prayer for Miss Armstrong, and a hymn?" After the prayer the women began to sing, "God be with you till we meet again."

The meeting continued with items of business that would not have pleased Annie. The delegates voted to continue the WMU headquarters in Baltimore, which was exactly the opposite of what Annie had wanted and had said would happen. They then increased the corresponding secretary's salary, in case the next woman actually accepted payment, and they appointed a committee to consider the advisability of starting a Woman's Missionary Union Training School in Louisville as soon as the WMU constitution allowed it. Fannie Heck was reelected as president. Mrs. Barker had stuck to her resolve not to serve again.

At the end of the meeting Mrs. Burnham asked that a rising vote of thanks be given to Annie. This was the same Mrs. Burnham who had been a Missouri delegate at the 1888 organizational meeting in Richmond. It was also the same Mrs. Burnham who had spoken for the training school at the 1905 Annual Meeting in Louisville and helped begin the confrontation that ended Annie's career.

Annie soon was reminded of the fickle nature of the public. Newspapers—sometimes the very ones that had so vehemently criticized her or supported the training school against her wishes—now sang her praises. The *Chattanooga Daily Times* said, "It would be impossible to pay too high a tribute to this noble godly woman who has so faithfully served her Master and the Baptist course in the south." The *Baptist and Reflector* said, "For twenty years she has guided the destinies of the Union. She has seen the contributions of the Union grow from nothing to about $100,000 a year. It is largely due to the Woman's Missionary Union that the contributions to Home and Foreign Missions have been considerably increased. It should be added that all of these years Miss Armstrong has served the Union without any salary."

And the *Religious Herald*, which had urged Virginia women to cooperate with the Louisville training school, apparently could not say enough to honor her, calling Annie "one of the most faithful, energetic, self-denying workers with whom the denomination has ever been blessed. Wonderfully alert and progressive, diligent and farseeing, she has seen the work prosper marvelously under her leadership. . . . Her name will always be a household word among Southern Baptists, and her memory will be frequent through the long years to come."

Her praises were sung by the Committee on Women's Work in its report to the SBC that year. The committee described Annie in glowing terms. "Possessed of a power to grasp and master details that amounts to genius; given a vision of the possibilities of organization and development among our people that few have ever had; having a love for souls amounting to a passion; loving God fervently and willing to make her life an unbroken day of sacrificial service to him, she has been to us and our work what few others could have been."

It was easy for Annie to believe that the praise and thanks, especially coming from those who had opposed her on the training school, were simply done for appearance' sake. After all, it cost little for a winner to be gracious to a defeated enemy. Was it possible, she wondered, that the overtures made by the likes of Mrs. Burnham and the *Religious Herald* were sincere, even made as a Christian gesture of reconciliation? Annie's character was not such that she could distinguish easily between rejection of her leadership and rejection of her personally. She needed time and a new work to which she could devote herself. With time, perhaps, she could learn to forgive.

11
Life After WMU

"Now, do you know your memory verse?" The austere woman bent down to look the little Sunday School student in the eye.

"Yes, Miss Annie," he said politely, and proceeded to recite. He missed only one word and started to sit back down, looking pleased with himself, only to be called back up by his teacher and told to recite perfectly. He sighed, but did as instructed. Miss Annie did not allow any sliding by on one's memory verses.

She was pleased at his perfect recitation, and he basked in the glow of her pleasure. Was this the Annie Armstrong that had helped forge WMU and then done battle with most of the SBC missions leaders? Not to the children gathered around her. To them she was the lady who taught them the Bible, showed them curios from her travels, listened to their stories, and encouraged their dreams. They could talk to her about anything.

"Are we still coming to tea at your house?" begged one little girl.

"Of course," their teacher said.

The children would have wiggled with anticipation, except Miss Annie didn't allow wiggling in Sunday School. But later, at her house, while dear Miss Alice served refreshments, they could admire her china and linen, laugh, and play games with her. And, if one had been very, very good, even be allowed to pull the food up on the amazing dumb waiter that ran from the kitchen to the upper room.

For Annie, one of the joys of leaving her WMU life was regaining her role as friend to the boys and girls of Eutaw Place. Now the days of heavy travel were behind her and she could stay close to her beloved family and church. She loved being the Primary Class secretary and drilling her little people in their memory work.

"Don't forget, tea at my house next week," she called as the children filed out. She made her way to the sanctuary for worship, making only a cool nod in the direction of Edith Campbell Crane, her successor as WMU corresponding secretary. She had no relationship with the WMU leaders, though she still attended the missionary society meetings. When they talked about supporting the training school she was silent, trying not to cause any friction. Well, it wasn't so bad. She had other things to busy herself with, such as the Home of the Friendless. She still taught Bible lessons to the children, and always showed up with a bag of stick candy.

The rest of the week passed as every week did now. More time to study the Bible, to read the Baptist newspapers (now that there was blessedly no more talk of her in them), and to spend with her adored family. She was coming back from a little visit with Mamie and her family when she passed a church member on the street.

"Don't forget Mothers' Meeting today, Annie," the woman called out. Annie was not likely to forget. She had presided over the Friday afternoon meetings since the 1880s whenever she was in town. She had started the meetings at Eutaw Place in the downstairs lecture room. The women who came were impoverished and often uneducated in both practical and spiritual matters. They would not attend worship services in such an intimidating church, but they would come for an informal meeting to get recipes, Bible study, and housekeeping tips.

Annie let herself in the front door of her house. Once again, they were without servants, so there was no one to meet her. Alice was resting. They had gotten up before daybreak to light the fires and do the other menial chores for the day. Now, though Annie was lagging from lack of sleep and her head ached, she began to gather her things for the mothers' meeting. She picked up her Bible and one of her many notebooks. "What a joke, for me to teach housekeeping," Annie thought. Everyone knew she was not interested in domestic matters, nor was she any good with them. Her household management tips were the result of study and discussions with Alice and other homemakers.

Today, the women would learn something about giving to others. Annie was determined that these women learn that they, too, had something to give to others. There was always someone in need, someone worse off than oneself. Being poor did not mean one had no Christian responsibilities. Not only would it teach the women to give to others, Annie knew that if the women could give to someone less fortunate, it would enhance their own sense of self-respect.

Annie entered the lecture room and greeted the women present. They were such a mishmash, she thought. Russians and Germans who had just been in the country a few months and women whose families had lived in Baltimore for generations. When they all started talking at once, good gracious, what a babble of accents! She looked around at them all, and realized again she loved them very much.

May 1907

"Here is a telegram for you, Miss Annie," called the servant girl. Annie strode to the door and took it with a sense of foreboding. Telegrams were often terrible news.

But this one was not. It came from the women of the WMU Annual Meeting in Richmond. It expressed their appreciation for all she had done with and for them. The telegram stirred a number of emotions within Annie, but she tried not to voice any of them.

She also discovered that at the Annual Meeting the women had taken bigger steps to honor her. From the money raised by WMU, SBC, they wished the boards to appropriate $5,000 each to raise memorials in her honor. Annie had already told the women she wished for no honors. She distinctly remembered saying, "That no words of thanks or recognition of her services be passed, as the record is on high." Perhaps the women felt that, since Annie herself had worked to honor Dr. Kerfoot and Dr. Tichenor with memorials, she wanted one herself. She could hardly appear ungrateful, but she decided to do nothing to encourage the matter.

She kept that resolution in July when Dr. Willingham wrote to her suggesting that the Yang Chow Hospital, the fund-raising for which had gotten her into so much trouble, be named for her.

"I am not asking whether you want us to put up a memorial for Southern Baptists will do that, and if you are not willing for them to do it while you live, they will after your death, but I think it is best for you to yield to the earnest wish of the sisters as well as of the brethren, and let us name some enterprise for you right away."

"Dear Dr. Willingham, I shall not answer your letter," Annie told him silently as she put it away. She stuck to her resolve, and Dr. Willingham, she found later, was reduced to writing a number of letters to Fannie Heck about the matter before Miss Heck told him he should have simply gone ahead and done it without consulting Annie. The Yang Chow Hospital never was named for her, which was quite all right with Annie.

But, she couldn't stop the Home Mission Board from naming a building at the Yancey Mountain School in Burnsville, North Carolina, in her honor. From Levering relatives that served on the WMU board and other friends Annie still learned quite a bit about WMU's doings. She knew that Edith Campbell Crane, Mrs. W. D. Chipley, and Mrs. Gray (the wife of the Home Mission Board secretary) represented WMU at the building dedication. WMU provided the inscribed tablet.

Annie was much more concerned, however, with the doings in Baltimore. There were so many immigrants, tens of thousands of them, and Baptists were doing so little to reach them! Her own neighborhood had changed from solely upper- and middle-class white families to include German immigrants, many of which were Jewish. Annie longed to share the gospel with all the immigrants, especially the Jewish community. She went to her friend who was an officer in a Union dedicated to sharing the gospel with Jews and offered her assistance.

When she wasn't supervising mothers' meetings at several churches, or entertaining visitors, or teaching Sunday School, Annie worked for the Home for Incurables, a large nursing home that had Eugene Levering as a benefactor. He and Mamie served on the board of directors. Annie sometimes thought of the long-ago days when she was a young girl and her mother was involved with the Union Protestant Infirmary. When Annie was feeling blue, she would visit the sick and seeing their troubles put her own into perspective. It still did.

December 21, 1915

Annie sat in stony silence looking out an upper-story window of her home. She should have been happy and busy preparing for a holiday dinner for the women at the mothers' meeting, or a party for the orphans. Instead, she sat with her Bible in her lap, a black dress shrouding her from neck to foot. Where was Alice? she wondered vaguely. Alice was in the house, puttering around the linen closet or kitchen probably, trying to soothe herself with work. But even work, Annie had found, did not ease all heartache.

Word had come to them that Mamie Armstrong Levering was dead. This news brought back reminders of other deaths. Dear Dr. Willingham had died just last year. The Foreign Mission Board debt had weighed on him so heavily that he suffered a fatal breakdown from the stress. Debt had killed him, as it had killed Lottie Moon. Annie still couldn't believe that the dynamic little woman she had shared the podium with at the 1903 Annual Meeting had died as she did, of starvation and mental stress. It was said Lottie Moon weighed only 50 pounds when she died on Christmas Eve 1912. She had given all her food to the starving Chinese, and worried herself into a frenzy over the Board's debt.

Even Fannie Heck was dead. She had succumbed to cancer in August of this year. Annie had made no attempt to reconcile with her, had not even sent a note to her sickroom. But still, she represented a part of Annie's past.

"The veil over the future is one of God's tenderest mercies," Annie reminded herself.

She looked down at the street and saw a family passing by. The neighborhood was changing again, and now many of her neighbors were black—doctors, teachers, ministers. It was always a middle-class neighborhood, but the complexion kept changing. Some of the children in the family looked up and waved at her. She waved back. Thank God, there were still people to love.

12
The Later Years

Baltimore, 1918

"It's so nice to have a wedding in the family again." The two sisters, now gray-haired but still tall and ramrod straight, were preparing for Eugene's marriage to Harriett Ellis. Alone for 3 years since Mamie's death, he had found a companion in Dr. Ellis's daughter. Not only was she the child of Annie's dear pastor and friend of WMU, Harriett was as devoted to missions as the Armstrong sisters and Eugene. She was a good match for him.

Regardless of what T. P. Bell and some others might say, Annie had nothing against marriage. She liked to see people happy. She looked at her sister's gentle face as she was busy about the household tasks and thought again how important her family was to her.

She roused herself from thoughts of family and weddings to get ready for the missions meeting at church. Although she refused to take any leadership role, Annie was faithful to attend the society. Today was an especially important meeting, since they would be discussing the annual Christmas offering for foreign missions.

She reached church on time, as usual, and greeted the women present. The only woman she was not friendly with was Kathleen Mallory, who had succeeded Edith

Campbell Crane as the WMU, SBC, corresponding secretary. As corresponding secretary, Edith had crumbled under a combination of delicate health, workload, and family responsibilities; and resigned to get married.

Annie did not quite know what to make of the dainty southern belle who had come from Alabama to lead the Union. She was so petite and quiet, always wore pastels, and had an undertone of quiet sorrow even when she was busy or cheerful. It was said that Kathleen Mallory had been engaged, and her sweetheart had died before the wedding. She had plunged into missions work as a remedy for grief. Annie did not delve into that subject. As an intensely private person herself, Annie respected privacy for others, even if she did slip unintentionally, as she did with Jessie Stakely's pregnancy.

The meeting came to order and the women started talking about the offering. During the talk, Annie made a suggestion which the other women took up immediately. "Should we not name the offering after our dear Miss Moon, who gave us the idea for the Christmas offering in the beginning?" It was hailed as an excellent idea, and at the next WMU, SBC, meeting the women of other states agreed. Because of Annie, the Lottie Moon Christmas Offering® for Foreign (now International) Missions formally came into being.

Baltimore, 1921–22
The Woman's Baptist Foreign Mission Society of Maryland was celebrating its Golden Jubilee. "How could it be 50 years? Where did the time go?" Annie asked herself. They had flown by with hard work and wonderful experiences, she knew. Maryland WMU had asked Annie, Alice, Mrs. Pollard, and Mrs. A. J. Rowland (the oldest living members of the society) to attend the celebration. The women even sang a hymn Alice wrote for the occasion. Kathleen Mallory was one of the guest speakers. This was

kind of her, since 1921 was a very busy year for her. The WMU national office was moving to Birmingham, Alabama, of all places.

In March 1922 Annie received a very nicely worded request from the WMU president, Mrs. Minnie Kennedy James. The Alabama WMU committee had suggested, and it was considered a good suggestion, that Annie furnish a picture of herself for the WMU national office. Annie had no more intention of giving them a picture than she had Dr. Willingham when he had asked so long ago. When he had finally tried to get tough and insisted on a picture, she sent one of her at her desk at the Maryland Mission Rooms—it was shot from the back. He got a nice view of Annie's hat, the back of her slender waist, and her chair. Mrs. James wasn't even going to get that much.

Baltimore, Fall 1928

The years were flying by. Annie still kept her interest in missions, as well as everything else. Now she had time to read, and not much else. Her health had started to fail and she had to give up much of her work, even leading the mother's meetings. But it was Alice that Annie was most concerned about.

Her darling sister had been in bed with lung problems for ten weeks, which had caused them to miss a special event. She, Alice, Mrs. Pollard, and Eliza Broadus had been invited to the 40-year anniversary of WMU, SBC, its Ruby Celebration. Alice, who could still wield her pen, had written a charming refusal. She explained that the doctor had said she could only go if he went, so of course his valet would come too, and a couple of nurses for Alice. She would really need to take her bed to be completely at ease.

"On the whole Annie and I think we will have to decline the gracious invitation and think of the happy times when it was our privilege to be there. We hope the

Ruby Celebration will be rich in blessings for today and the days to follow."

The sisters could, at least, talk of those good times with WMU. The time for holding on to the bitter memories was past. Now there should be just the sweet memories to think of. Their reminiscences were broken by a delivery. Maryland WMU had marked the Ruby Celebration by sending a bouquet to the sisters, and a picnic basket full of delicious goodies. Annie smiled when she saw the flowers selected: roses and forget-me-nots.

Those good memories helped the sisters through a fresh grief that was soon to follow. Eugene died, just one month after retiring from his office at the bank. He was 82, and had been the closest thing to a brother they had since their own brothers were dead or missing.

But that blow was only a shadow of what was to come. On December 15, Alice went to be with their parents and Mamie in heaven. She could not overcome her lung problems. After 78 years, Annie was alone.

She would no longer stay in the row house on McCulloh Street. It held 60 years of memories, but it was time to leave. On a practical level, there was no sense in staying in a big house alone . . . all alone. Annie moved into the Cecil Apartments, which adjoined Eutaw Place. She could walk right next door to church. Yes, she would be fine.

Cecil Apartments, Baltimore 1929–31

The days of preparing Christmas parties for the orphans and turkey dinners for the mothers' meetings were over. That was no reason, Annie thought, not to keep extending hospitality at the holidays. There was a nice young man, Clyde Atkins, who on New Year's Day would begin as associate pastor at Eutaw Place. But now here it was Christmas, and his wife was in the hospital having their baby. How lost the young man must be! He should have dinner with her.

W. Clyde Atkins, only 26 years old, was happy to accept the invitation. He had an excellent dinner with Miss Armstrong, who was kind and caring to him. The meal was cleared away and she turned her still-piercing gaze on him.

"Now," she said in a strong voice. "Your place is with your wife at the hospital." He couldn't agree more and prepared to go. "One more thing," Miss Armstrong added. "May I claim the privilege of giving you and your wife a carriage for your baby boy?" He didn't know if it was the meal, the kindness, or the words *baby boy* that won him over, but Clyde Atkins quickly formed a strong attachment to Annie Armstrong.

Other people had attachments to Annie, too. Eugene's widow, Harriett, moved into the Cecil Apartments in 1931. Annie had other friends there, too. And, she had moved from Infant Class teacher to Berean Class teacher. The Berean Class was made up of the older women in the church. She still attended the mothers' meetings when she could.

Cecil Apartments, 1930s

Annie sat in her apartment, idly looking at a magazine. There were books and journals all over the apartment, open for reading or with her place marked in them. But she couldn't read today. She had a decision to make, and there was no one to help her.

The WMU, SBC, Executive Committee had asked her permission to name the March offering for home missions in her honor. Annie was still put off by earthly honors, so the women had argued it would help promote the offering. But this was 1934, the country was in the Great Depression. If it meant more money for home missions . . .

She agreed, and the Annie Armstrong Easter Offering® for Home (now North American) Missions was launched.

Annie gradually declined physically until by 1936 she was confined to her bed. She still had many visitors, and her mind stayed sharp. One day she was thrilled with a visit from a cousin who had gone to China as a missionary and was home on furlough. She and her husband visited by Annie's bedside.

"I hope your bed is comfortable, Cousin Annie," he said politely.

"What kind of bed do the Chinese women have?" she shot back. She still wanted to know what was going on in missions and the world. She had even reached the point where she was hungry for news of the training school, and wasn't embarrassed to ask how it was doing.

When spring came to Baltimore, Annie looked out the window and thought of the days when she and the other children played in the parks and streets. Children certainly couldn't play in Baltimore's streets now the way they did back then.

"Miss Annie, you have visitors," the servant announced. Harriett Levering and Juliette Mather of WMU came into the room. After some small talk, they asked if Annie had greetings she wished to send to the 50th anniversary of WMU, SBC, which would be held in Richmond in May. Yes, she certainly did.

"My message for the Union in its 50th year is that I hope it may grow every year stronger and better. I would link with this thought the Scripture verse: 'Speak unto the children of Israel that they go forward.'

"For the young women in YWA my wish is that they 'grow in grace and in the knowledge of our Lord and Savior Jesus Christ.'

"Do the Girls' Auxiliary members know the two verses most often read and committed to memory?—'For God so loved the world that he gave His only begotten Son that whosoever believeth on Him should not perish but have eternal life. . . . The Lord is my Shepherd.'

"Tell the Royal Ambassadors to 'be strong in the Lord and in the power of His might.' I can say with emphasis that I have found this verse to be true.

"My message for the Sunbeams is the Shepherd Psalm.

"To encourage you in your special offerings for missions I would say: 'Blessed are ye that sow beside the waters.' Water suggests expansion and growth. After study of God's word comes study of the fields. Then people pray. Then they give.'"

This was Annie's first official word to WMU since 1906. Kathleen Mallory paid tribute to her at the meeting, and the women there felt honored to hear from Annie. Though Annie could not go to Richmond, the women sent their love to her with a bouquet of golden roses.

November came, and with it the Maryland WMU Annual Meeting. Kathleen Mallory conveyed to Annie the greetings of the Maryland women and brought her greetings back to them. The women were delighted to have a personal message from her.

It was one of the last personal messages anyone would receive. Annie now drifted in and out of a coma. "My boys! My boys!" she called frequently, when in her mind she was still a young woman teaching her Infant Class Sunday School. W. Clyde Atkins, now pastor of Eutaw Place, heard that "her boys" were on Annie's mind. He saw a chance to show a last kindness to the woman who had been so kind to him one lonely Christmas Day.

"Miss Annie," he called gently. "Miss Annie, I have brought you a visitor." Annie opened her eyes and saw Pastor Atkins and a strapping young college student by his side. Her mind cleared and she recognized one of her little boys, now grown to be a fine man. She smiled.

"Now, do you know your memory verse?" she whispered.

"Yes, Miss Annie," he replied obediently, and began to recite the verses she had taught him so perfectly in Sunday

School. Miss Annie recited them with him, and they even sang the old songs together. Then, she sagged. The strength she had gained from the excitement of his visit was gone.

"Will you each pray?" she asked. The young man and Pastor Atkins both said a prayer, and bade her a fond good-bye.

On December 20, 1938, Annie Armstrong laid down the work of a lifetime and went to the reward waiting her. Two days later, a small group of family held her funeral service at her apartment. Pastor Atkins officiated, and F. F. Briggs, a relative, said the prayer. Annie's body was then laid to rest in the family plot at Green Mount Cemetery. On her grave marker would be put words from one of Annie's personal notebooks: "She hath done what she could."

There must be more done for her than that private service, Southern Baptists said. Too many people wished to honor Annie's memory to leave it at that. On January 29, 1939, Eutaw Place Baptist Church overflowed with people coming to pay tribute to her. Former pastors, WMU and Southern Baptist leaders, representatives of the local institutions where she was benefactor, black Baptist leaders, and missionaries all drew together to remember the woman who had urged them always to go forward.

Pastor Atkins had many wonderful things to say of the woman who had been a Southern Baptist leader as well as his personal friend. He praised her vision and her practicality. She had, he said, the clear-eyed ability to see needs close to home and also far away, and wanted to meet them both. She had many dreams, but was a dreamer in action. She was "one who dreamed her dreams and then made her dreams come true."

In the next WMU Executive Committee, national president Ethlene Boone Cox paid tribute to Annie Armstrong. Among the words she said were ones that would have pleased Annie, not because of their reflection on her, but their effect on others.

Mrs. Cox said, "Her life and service are a challenge to each of us to give her best." This was what Annie had asked of herself and of everyone around her: to give her best for the kingdom of God.

Epilogue

What made Annie Walker Armstrong one of the most revered leaders among Southern Baptist women? It was not just her almost inhuman ability to work, though her capacity for work was staggering. That ability to work left a legacy that shaped Southern Baptist life. Weeks of prayer, missionary boxes (now called Christmas in August), offerings, church building loan funds, annuities, work with language and ethnic groups, young people's work, local ministries—she left her imprint on all these things. But that was not the source of her greatness.

Nor was it her personality. When one reads of her relationships with other leaders, the impression given is not always a nice one. Annie could be stubborn and even petty. Again and again, Annie started off with a warm regard for someone, only to find the relationship cooling (for example, T. P. Bell, Fannie Heck, Jessie Stakely, Dr. Frost, and Martha McIntosh Bell). Each time Annie felt the person had wronged her, but she had her own part in the breakup.

Like many strong-minded people, it seemed that peer relationships were hardest for her to navigate. To everyone else—children, the women in the churches, the black women led by Nannie Helen Burroughs, her family—she was both charming and helpful. Was she a split personality? Was she putting on an act? No. She led at a time when society, especially Christian society, loaded women with burdens heavy to be borne. The woman leader must be feminine, modest, retiring, and charming. If that were all she were, however, she would never last as leader. She had to be able to withstand the criticisms of the state Baptist papers and the physical rigors of hard work and travel; be knowledgeable in finances, administration, and parliamentary procedure, all the while balancing multiple demands on her time.

And, she had a personal life, too. Many people have speculated on who asked Annie to marry and why the marriage didn't take place. Annie's family members later reported that while a few relatives knew, Annie had not wanted the fact broadcast. If it had been Rosewell Graves or J. B. Hartwell, both of whom married friends of Annie's, it's easy to see why she wouldn't want the fact known. It would have been terribly awkward for all concerned.

But though she did not marry, she did have a family, a large one. She related to her sisters and her nieces and nephews. She cared for an ailing, elderly parent. That fact is often overlooked, as is the influence of that family, from her mother to her sister Alice to her cousins Eugene and Joshua Levering.

If it was not work or family or personality that made Annie what she was, what was it? Why did she achieve so much when other women merely dabbled in Christian service? Most who have studied her life would agree it was her spiritual depth and her faith. She was a real person, with faults and flaws and little character quirks. Yet she became great because she knew the promises of the Scriptures and believed them. She knew God would give a woman—any woman—power to endure and triumph when her heart is set only on serving God. Many women have given lip service to that idea. Annie based her life on it, and that is what made the difference.

Thank you!

Your purchase of this book and other WMU products supports the mission and ministries of WMU. To find more great resources, visit our online store at www.wmustore.com or talk with one of our friendly customer service representatives at 1-800-968-7301.

WMU®
Discover the Joy of Missions[SM]
www.wmu.com